LAND OF THE GREAT LAKES

Illustrations in color by WARREN CHASE MERRITT

Land of the
GREAT LAKES

CHARLES E. HOWELL
Professor of Social Science
Northern Illinois University
De Kalb, Illinois

PAUL SEEHAUSEN
Professor of Education
Valparaiso University
Valparaiso, Indiana

THELMA SHAW
Teacher-Author
Chicago, Illinois

HARR WAGNER PUBLISHING COMPANY · San Francisco

TABLE OF CONTENTS

A STORY ABOUT A STORY

"Tell us a story," said Linda and David to their father one night.

"I will tell you how stories happen, if you like," their father answered.

"Do you mean you are going to tell a story about a story?" Linda wanted to know.

"That's right," said Father. "Not all stories happened a long time ago. Stories are happening now. Stories are happening all the time."

"Today I told Allan about the sheep that jumped over Grandfather's fence," said David. "Did that make a story?"

"Yes," said Mr. Cook. "Maybe you will remember it and tell it to your little boy or girl a long time from now. By then it will be a long-ago story."

"Is that all a story is?" asked David. "Is it just something that happened to somebody?"

"That's what a true story is. True stories about what happened long ago are called 'history.' Listen. If you say 'history' slowly, it sounds like 'his story.'"

"Oh, yes," said David. "Stories about the country we live in are called history."

"The teacher showed us a map today," said Linda. "She showed us where we live. Are there stories about the part where we live?"

"Yes," said Mr. Cook. "There are many stories about our great

1

Middle West. That is what most people call this part of the country. Another name is the Land of the Great Lakes. Tomorrow we will look at a map like the one Linda's teacher has. Then I will tell you stories about some of the places near our own home."

THINGS TO TALK ABOUT

1. What happened in school last week that could be a story?
2. What are some of the long-ago stories that you know?
3. How can long-ago stories be of help to us today?

SOMETHING TO DO

Write a very short story about something that happened to you.

A STORY ABOUT A MAP

The next night the children asked their father for a story about the Land of the Great Lakes.

"I want to learn about the place where I live," said David.

"I would like to have you show me places on the map," said Linda. "I have a hard time finding them by myself."

"Let's make a map," said Father. "First we will put down a mark to show where we are."

Mr. Cook took a big piece of paper and put an X on it. "That is where we are," he said. "Now let's put a mark at the top of the paper. That will show something that is north of us. Then we'll put a mark at the bottom of the paper, to show something to the south of us. There!"

The paper looked like this.

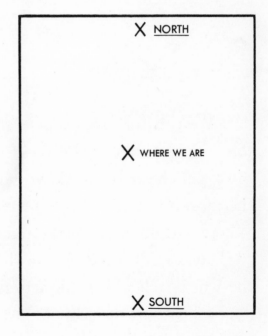

"If we look to the north, the sun comes up over there." Father waved his right hand. He was facing north. Then he turned back to the little map he had just made.

"Then this must be the west, where the sun goes down." This time he waved his left hand because he was still facing north.

Mr. Cook put two more marks on the paper.

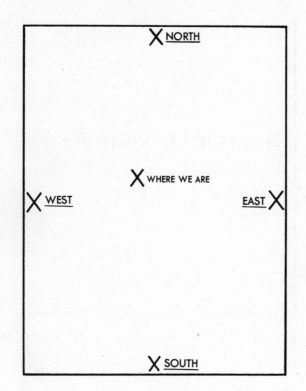

Now the map looked like this.

"We can use this map to show where anything is," Mr. Cook told the children. "The farther away the thing is, the farther we must put the mark to show where it is. When you go to school in the morning, the sun is in your eyes. You know you are going east. Where is the school on the map?"

David made an X on the right side of the map. Beside it he put the word "school" in big letters.

"That's for our school," he said.

Now Linda wanted the pencil. "When we go to church, we go the other way. Let me put a mark on the left side, for the church."

"Remember that the church is farther from our house than the school is," her father said. "Put the mark a little farther away."

Then they made another mark, closer to the house but up near the top of the paper. David put the word "store" up there.

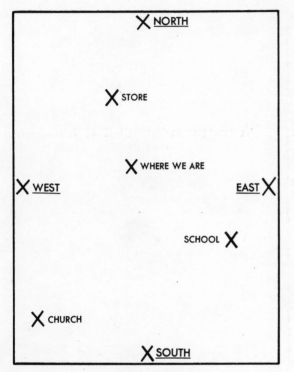

Now their map looked like this.

"All maps begin in this same way," said Mr. Cook. "Even a map with many, many places on it. Look at this big one I brought home to show you."

Together they looked at the big map. Down in one corner there were some words that David could read. The words were "Land of the Great Lakes."

"Look," said Linda. "There are five big blue places for the five Great Lakes."

Linda and David together read out loud the names of the five lakes. They are

> Superior
> Huron
> Michigan
> Erie
> Ontario.

"We are lucky to live in a place where there are so many lakes," said David. "There are many more besides the five Great Lakes."

"That's true," his father answered. "There are hundreds of lakes in the Middle West."

They tried to count all the lakes on their big map, but it was bedtime before they were half through.

"Thank you for the map story," said Linda over her shoulder as she started up the stairs.

"There are some funny names on that map," called David from his room. "Tell us a story about them tomorrow."

THINGS TO TALK ABOUT

1. How does the sun help you to remember where "north" is?
2. Why do people need to know how to use maps?
3. Some maps of the world are like big round balls. Have you ever seen such maps? What are they called?

SOMETHING TO DO

Make a map like Linda's and David's. Show where you live and where your school is. Show a store and a friend's house.

A STORY ABOUT NAMES

Dinner was over. David spread out a big map on the table. "Please tell us a story about these funny names," he asked his father.

"There are many Indian names in our Land of the Great Lakes," said his father. "They are not funny names. They seem funny because you don't know what they mean."

Linda pointed to a place on the map. "There is Chicago," she said. "We live in Chicago. Is Chicago an Indian name?"

"Yes, it is," her father told her. "Chicago means 'wild onion.'"

"It's hard to believe that wild onions used to grow here," said David. "Chicago is the biggest city in the state of Illinois. Is Illinois an Indian name, too?"

"Yes," said Mr. Cook. "Illinois got its name from a tribe of Indians. A tribe was like a very, very large family. The town of Muncie, Indiana, is named for another family of Indians. They were called wolf Indians. Muncie means 'land of the wolf.'"

"I can guess about Indiana!" cried Linda. "Indiana is just the word 'Indian' with the letter 'a' at the end!"

"Good for you!" said Father. "It's a name the Americans made up."

David shut his eyes and put his finger on the map. Then he opened his eyes. "I am pointing at Milwaukee, Wisconsin," he said. "What do those names mean?"

"Milwaukee means 'good place,'" his father answered. "No one is sure about Wisconsin. Some people think it means 'a meeting of the waters.'"

8

"That sounds right," said Linda. "There are lots of lakes and rivers in Wisconsin."

"There are in Minnesota, too!" David pointed at Minnesota on the map. "I know what Minnesota means. It means 'land of sky-blue waters.' "

"That's a pretty name," said Linda. "So is Ohio. I like to say 'Ohio.' It has a pretty sound."

"The sound makes me think of a boat on a river," Mr. Cook said with a smile. "Ohio means 'the great river' or 'the beautiful river.' "

"How about Michigan?" David wondered. "That's a hard one to say."

"The real Indian name was even harder," his father said. "It was *Mitchisawyegan*. That was the Indian word for 'great lake.' "

David remembered the story about names when he went to bed that night. "I'm glad we don't have to use that long Indian name any more," he thought to himself. " 'Land of the Great Lakes' is easy to say."

He tried to think how the Indians would have said "Land of the Great Lakes." But he fell asleep instead.

THINGS TO TALK ABOUT

1. Can you think of some other Indian names we use today?
2. What is the name of the street where you live? Can you guess how it got its name?

SOMETHING TO DO

Find your state on the map. Pick out the name of a town in your state. Find out how that town got its name. Tell the class.

EAST OR WEST, HOME IS BEST

David was waiting at the door when his father came home the next evening.

"Dad," said David, "Mother says you can count miles on a map. How do you do it?"

"Wait a minute!" laughed his father. "Give me a chance to hang up my hat! Find a ruler while you are waiting, if you want to."

When David had the ruler, his father spread the map on the floor. They got down on their knees to look at it. "What miles do you want to count?" asked Mr. Cook.

"Uncle Ed lives in New York. That's in the East. How far is New York from the Land of the Great Lakes?" David asked.

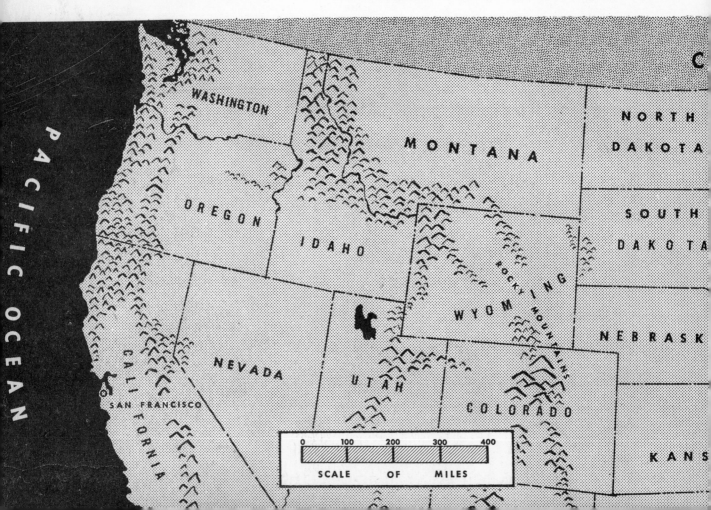

"Let's line up the ruler between New York City and the Great Lakes country," said his father. He helped David lay the ruler on the map.

"But the ruler doesn't show how many miles," said David.

"Right," his father answered. "But look in this corner of the map. Here is a line with numbers on it. This is called a scale of miles. Measure with the ruler on the map. Then put the ruler on the scale of miles."

David looked at the ruler. One end was on the place marked "New York." He put his finger on the part of the ruler that was on the edge of the Great Lakes country. He kept his finger there, but he moved the ruler to the scale of miles.

"What number on the scale does your finger point to now?" asked Father.

"Just about 300," answered David. "Does that mean I measured 300 miles?"

"Yes," said Mr. Cook. "The line on the map is just as long as the line marked 300 on the scale. That means the line on the map covers 300 miles."

"What if I measure all the way from New York City to Chicago?" asked David. "That would be more than 300 miles."

"It would be more than 700," said Mr. Cook.

Just then Linda came in. She wanted to know what her father and brother were doing. When they told her, she said, "Measure how far it is from Chicago to California. How many miles is it to San Francisco, where Grandma lives?"

"That's far," said David. "That's out west." He began to measure. He had to use the 300 mark on the scale six times. Then he still had space left over.

"That is far," said Linda. "Uncle Ed lives a long way to the east, in New York. But Grandma lives many more miles away, in the West. We are not in the middle at all."

"No, we aren't," said her brother. "Why is the Land of the Great Lakes called the Middle West? It is not in the middle at all!"

Mr. Cook laughed. "You are right," he said. "But once upon a time the Land of the Great Lakes was the Far West of our country."

"I like once-upon-a-time stories," said Linda. She sat down to listen.

"Once this Land of the Great Lakes belonged to England," Mr. Cook went on. "Very few white men lived here then. This was Indian country. No one knew much about the land to the west of the Mississippi River." He showed the children that river on the map.

"Then the part where we live was the West!" said David.

"In a way, yes," his father answered. "But it did not stay that way. Many things happened. England gave up the land all the way to the Mississippi. Our country began to be called the United States. People who lived in the United States began to move west. Soon the United States owned land all the way to the Rocky Mountains."

"I see the Rocky Mountains," said David. He pointed to them on the map.

"Oh!" cried Linda. "Then those mountains were the West! Then the Land of the Great Lakes was in the middle!"

"That is when people began to call it the Middle West," her father told her. "Midwest is another name for Middle West."

"How many states are in the Midwest?" asked David.

"How many states are in the Land of the Great Lakes?" asked Linda at the same time.

"Let's answer Linda's question," said Father. "That way we won't have so many states to count before dinner!"

So they counted, one by one, on the map.

> Minnesota.
> Wisconsin.
> Michigan.
> Illinois.
> Indiana.
> Ohio.

"Good!" said Mr. Cook. "Those states are all in the Midwest. They are all part of the Land of the Great Lakes, besides. Talking about those six states will keep us busy for a while."

Linda was still looking at the map. "East or west, home is best," she said.

When they laughed, she said, "Well, that's what Grandma says!"

"That's a fine way to feel," said her father. "Grandma feels that way, and she lives in the West. Uncle Ed feels that way, and he lives in the East."

"And we feel that way," said David, "because we live in the Land of the Great Lakes."

"Daddy," said Linda, "I want you to tell us all the stories there are about the Land of the Great Lakes."

"That would be a lot of stories," said her father, smiling, "but I'll do my best."

THINGS TO TALK ABOUT

1. Have you ever taken a long trip in a car? Did the driver of the car use a map? What are some of the things a driver can find out by looking at a map?
2. How would you make a measuring scale to use with a map of your room?
3. How did the Middle West get its name?

SOMETHING TO DO

Get a large map. Stick a pin in the map to mark the place where you live. Stick another pin in the map to mark a city in another state. Use the scale of miles to find out how many miles there are between those two places.

Maps have marks on them to show cities, rivers, lakes, roads, and many other things. Look at a highway map of your state. On a piece of paper, draw as many of these "map marks" as you can find. After each picture, write what the mark stands for.

14

All the stories in this book are true stories. They are all stories about the Land of the Great Lakes. David and Linda liked every one of them. They hope you will, too.

IN THE DAYS OF LONG AGO

THE BEAUTIFUL SILK COAT

The land called France is many, many miles east from our Land of the Great Lakes. France is in Europe, across the Atlantic Ocean.

The large land called China is many, many miles west of the Great Lakes. China is in Asia, across the Pacific Ocean.

But France and China and our Great Lakes are all part of a story about a coat.

The coat belonged to a man named Jean Nicolet. Jean lived in France. He wanted to go to China.

People sometimes went to China from Europe long ago. In those days it was a long, hard trip. There were no cars or trains or airplanes then. The people went part way by ship. Then they would ride horses for many, many miles. After that, they had to cross a desert.

A desert is a place where there is very little water. Horses could not go far without water. The people had to ride camels instead. A camel is an animal that can travel many days without a drink of water.

At last the people from Europe would reach the rich countries of the East. There were many things in those rich countries that they could not get in Europe. There were some things in Europe that the countries of the East did not have. The people from Europe traded with the people of the East.

The traders who made that long, hard trip brought back beautiful things. They brought silk from China. They also brought ginger, cinnamon, and other spices. But each trip kept them away from home for years!

Nicolet thought there must be a better way to go to China. In those days the traders traveled east from Europe to reach China. Nicolet thought it would be better to go west. He thought he could cross North America and find China that way.

Nicolet came to North America with a man named Champlain. Champlain worked for the king of France.

"I have heard of a land of many lakes," Champlain told Nicolet one day. "It is said that the people there are different from any other people we have seen. The king of France wants to know more about those people and their land. Will you go to visit them?"

"Oh, yes!" said Nicolet. He was very happy. He was sure the land of many lakes was China!

"I wonder what kind of clothes I should take," thought Nicolet. "When I get to China I want to dress the way people there are dressed."

Nicolet had a fine silk coat. The silk had come from China.

The coat had pictures of birds and flowers on it. The pictures were part of the cloth.

"I will take my China coat!" said Nicolet.

He packed the silk coat carefully in his birch-bark canoe. The coat he was wearing was one made of deerskin.

Nicolet, with some Indians to help him, paddled up the St. Lawrence River. He took his canoe into the waters of Lake Ontario, Lake Erie, and Lake Huron. He paddled into Lake Michigan. No white man had ever been on that great lake before!

Nicolet and his helpers traveled for many days without seeing anyone. At last they came to a place where people were living. Nicolet could see the smoke from their fires.

"This might be China!" said Nicolet to himself. "I will put on my China coat."

Moving carefully, so as not to upset the canoe, he took out the fine silk coat. He put it on over his other clothes. Just to be on the safe side, he also took a pistol in each hand.

Now he was ready! Now he would land at China!

Of course he was not near China. He was in part of the Land of the Great Lakes. Nicolet had reached what is now Green Bay, Wisconsin.

But, as things turned out, Nicolet was glad he had put on that fine silk coat. The Green Bay Indians had never seen a white man before. They might have been afraid. They might have tried to kill Nicolet because they were afraid of him.

Instead, they fell in love with his coat! It was so beautiful that they could think of little else.

Nicolet let the Indians touch the flowers and birds that were part of the cloth. He let them feel the silk.

19

"This man must have come from the sky!" the Indians told one another. "We have never seen a man like this on earth before!"

Nicolet traveled among these Indians for a whole year. They told him many things about their land of the great lakes.

"There is a great water over there," said the Indians, pointing to the west. "It is very long. It has no end."

"That must be the China Sea," thought Nicolet. He still thought that he was close to China.

Today, of course, we know what the water was. It was the Mississippi River!

20

Nicolet never did reach China. His dreams did not come true. But he was a brave man. We remember him for many reasons.

He was the first white man to travel by canoe on Lake Michigan. He was the first white man to visit what is now Wisconsin. He was the only man about whom people said, "He put on a fine silk coat to visit the Green Bay Indians."

THINGS TO TALK ABOUT

1. Why did people from Europe make the long, hard trip to China?
2. What are some of the countries they may have crossed on their way to China? Remember they went by ship, on horseback, and on camels. You may look at a map or globe while you talk about this.
3. What are some of the things we get from other countries today?
4. Why did the king of France want to learn about the land of many lakes?

SOMETHING TO DO

Look at a map or globe of the world. Find France and China on it. Draw a make-believe line with your finger. Make the line show how Nicolet could have come from France to North America. Draw another make-believe line to show how far China is from Wisconsin.

On a map of North America, draw a make-believe line to show Nicolet's canoe trip. He started from a place on the St. Lawrence River that is called Three Rivers.

TWO FRIENDS FIND A RIVER

Once upon a time Indians were the only people in the Land of the Great Lakes. Later on, a few brave men sailed across the Atlantic Ocean. Some of them came to this rich new land.

One of these brave men was Father Marquette. He left his home in France. He came to the Land of the Great Lakes to be a teacher to the Indians. In a very short time he learned to speak six different Indian languages.

Father Marquette went to live among the Indians at St. Ignace in Michigan. He loved the Indians, and he loved their wild country. Some of his Indian friends told him about a great river called the Mississippi. Father Marquette wished that he could visit all the Indians who lived beside that river.

One day a young fur trader came to see Father Marquette.

"My name is Louis Joliet," the young man told him. "I am a trapper and a fur trader. The governor of Canada has sent me to see you. He wants you and me to go to the Mississippi River. He wants us to find out all we can about the land along that river."

"This is an answer to my prayers!" cried Father Marquette. "Let us get ready to go!"

Marquette and Joliet took five other men to help them. They had two birch canoes, which they paddled along the northern shores of Lake Michigan. Each night they stopped and built a campfire. They ate smoked meat and Indian corn.

Soon Marquette and Joliet came to the Menomonie River, in

what is now Wisconsin. There they made friends with the Indians. Those Indians were called the wild-rice Indians.

The wild-rice Indians wanted the white men to stay with them. "You will be safe with us," the red men said. "If you go on you may be killed."

But the brave men went on. They went to what is now Green Bay, and into the Fox River. Often they came to falls in the river. Then they had to walk for miles, carrying their canoes.

The little party of men crossed Lake Winnebago. They followed the Winnebago River and carried their canoes to the Wisconsin River. At last, near what is now Prairie du Chien, Wisconsin, they reached the Mississippi.

For two long weeks they paddled down the river. They saw no people anywhere. Then one day they saw the footprints of a man on shore!

Marquette and Joliet set out alone to find the man who had made that footprint. They saw a path and followed it. It led them to an Indian village.

The two friends were very quiet until they were quite close to the wigwams. Then they made a lot of noise so the Indians would come outside. Marquette and Joliet did not know whether these were friendly Indians or not.

Four Indian braves walked forward. They held peace pipes with pretty feathers on them. Then the white men knew that these were friendly Indians.

The Indians gave a party for the white men. The Indian women cooked corn and fish and dog and buffalo meat. A young Indian man fed the visitors. Sometimes he fed them with his fingers! He would not let Marquette and Joliet feed themselves at all.

The next morning Marquette and Joliet went back to their canoes. Before they left, the Indian chief gave Marquette a present. It was a pipe of peace.

"Show this to other Indians you meet," the old chief said. "They will know you are our friends. They will be kind to you."

He was right.

Marquette and Joliet went on down the Mississippi. They went past the place where the Missouri River rushes into the Mississippi. They went past a forest that stood where the city of St. Louis is today. They went past the mouth of the Ohio River. Then one day they saw more Indians!

At first the white men were afraid. The Indians were afraid, too. But then Marquette remembered the peace pipe. He held it up.

When they saw the peace pipe, the Indians were not afraid. They let the white men come ashore. Again there was a party. The Indians gave their visitors buffalo meat and bear oil and white plums.

Marquette and Joliet stopped at two more Indian villages along the banks of the Mississippi. Always the Indians gave the white men food. Always the white men gave the Indians beads and bits of cloth and other presents.

Everywhere they stopped Marquette was able to talk to the Indians. He asked them questions about the great river. The answers the Indians gave were not always right. The Indians did not know much about the river either.

There were Indians living near the mouth of the Arkansas River. They told Marquette and Joliet that the south end of the great river was nearby. This was not true. The Mississippi runs into the Gulf of Mexico, and that was 700 miles away.

Marquette and Joliet did not know that. They thought they had traveled along most of the river. They thought their job was done. They did not want to go the rest of the way.

Another country, Spain, had sent men to the land near the Gulf of Mexico. Spain and France both wanted the same land. Marquette and Joliet had made their long, hard trip for France. The men from Spain might kill them and throw away the maps that they had made. If that happened, all the work the two friends had done would have been for nothing. It was better to turn back while they were safe.

The brave travelers went along the Illinois River on their way back. From there they went to Lake Michigan. They stayed for a while at the very place where the city of Chicago is today.

Marquette and Joliet were two brave men. They learned many things about the Mississippi. They helped other men to find out more

25

about the great river. They helped the Land of the Great Lakes to grow. Long ago they began to make the Middle West a pleasant place to live.

THINGS TO TALK ABOUT

1. Why did people from across the ocean come to the Land of the Great Lakes so long ago?
2. Why did Father Marquette need to know many Indian languages?
3. Why were Marquette and Joliet good men to send along the river?
4. What towns and cities might Marquette and Joliet see if they made their trip today?
5. Talk about the reasons why Marquette and Joliet turned back before they reached the mouth of the Mississippi. Do you think they were right to turn back? Take a vote on this.
6. Marquette and Joliet visited a place where Nicolet had been many years before. What was the name of it? Can you find it on a map?

SOMETHING TO DO

Act out a play about Marquette and Joliet and their men. Show how they made friends with the Indians. Show how the Indians were kind to the white men.

On a map of Wisconsin, find every river and lake on which Marquette and Joliet traveled before they turned back.

On a map of the United States, find the place where Marquette and Joliet stopped and turned back.

Make a peace pipe out of soap or modeling clay.

WHITE SON OF THE RED MEN

One spring day almost three hundred years ago, three men started on a trip. They packed a canoe with presents for the Indians they might meet along the way. Then they started down the Illinois River, from about where Peoria is today.

One of these men was called Father Hennepin. Father Hennepin loved to write stories. He wrote stories about the things that happened on the trip. Some of the stories are true. Some are not true. It is hard for us to tell, so many years later, which are the true stories. Most people think that this story is true:

Hennepin and his two friends stopped one day to fix their canoe. While they were working on it, a big war party of Indians came along. There were more than a hundred Indians.

Some of the Indians wanted to kill the three white men. Others wanted to be friends.

"Let's split his head with a war club," said one of the chiefs. He looked at Hennepin when he said it. He made signs, so that Hennepin would be sure to understand.

"Let's not kill any of them," said another. "We want French traders to come among us. We can get knives and guns and hatchets from French traders. If we kill these white men, other white men will not come to trade with us."

"Let's start for home," a third chief said. "We can make up our minds on the way."

So the Indians started for home, taking the white men with them.

Hennepin's canoe was heavy and slow. Indian warriors helped the white men to paddle it. On fair nights, the whole party slept under the stars. When it rained, they slept in huts made from tree branches. Sometimes they stopped to have a bear or buffalo hunt. Then they went on again.

They passed beautiful Lake Pepin. After almost three weeks of travel they landed near what is now St. Paul.

There the Indians hid their canoes. Then they went on foot, all the way north to what is now Mille Lacs.

The Indians were tall and strong. Hennepin could not keep up with them. But the Indians found a way to make him move faster. They set fire to the grass behind him! Then, taking him by the hands, they ran forward with him, ahead of the flames.

Once in a while they came to a stream too deep to walk across. Then they had to swim. Hennepin's friends did not know how to swim. The Indians swam with the white men on their backs.

At last they reached the Indian town. The houses there were made of poles. There were poles for the roof and thick poles for the sides. Each house was covered with bark from the elm trees.

Indian women fed the tired, hungry men. They gave each man a large dish made of birch bark. The dishes were filled with wild rice and dried wild berries. Hennepin liked the food. He had not had such a good meal for a long time.

Then the Indians began to talk about the three white men. Should they be killed? Or should they be given to three different Indian families?

At last a tall chief turned to Hennepin. "You come with me," he said. "You are my son now!"

So, tired as he was, Hennepin had to start walking again. He and his new "father" walked to a lake a few miles away. The tall chief lived on an island in the middle of the lake. Some women of his tribe were waiting with canoes. They took Hennepin and his "father" to the island. Hennepin's two friends were taken to other villages.

Hennepin lived among the Indians for many months. The Indians did not have much food, but they shared it with him. He, in turn, helped them when they were sick. He showed them things they had never seen before, too. He showed them a compass that he carried with him. The Indians were a little bit afraid of the compass. They could not see how a compass knew which way was north!

The Indians were kind enough. But they would not let Hennepin go away from them. At last he said, "If you will not let me go alone, come with me. We will go back to the Mississippi River. We will find white men there. They will give us food."

Of course Hennepin was not sure they would meet white men. He only hoped they would! But the Indians believed him. A large party of Indians got ready for the trip. They took Hennepin's two friends along, too.

Down the Rum River, one after another, floated the canoes. When they reached the Mississippi, the Indians made camp on the side of a hill. Some put up tents made from animal skin. Some built little bark houses.

The Indian men carried clubs of stone and arrows with stone heads. They used these things for hunting.

The Indian women had knives of stone. They used the knives to cut up pieces of dried meat. They cooked the meat in pans made from dried mud. They made the pans themselves.

When the camp was finished, Hennepin said, "Now let me go to find the white men."

One of Hennepin's friends wanted to stay with the Indians. The other one went with Hennepin. The two men started out alone in a birch-bark canoe. They took with them only a gun, a knife, and a pan for cooking.

They followed the Mississippi. Near what are now the cities of St. Paul and Minneapolis they came to a great waterfall. Hennepin named the place the Falls of St. Anthony. The falls are still there, but they are much smaller now than when Hennepin saw them.

Hennepin and his friend carried their canoe around the falls. Then they went on down the river.

It was hard to find food along the way. The two friends killed a deer, but they did not know how to dry the meat. The weather was hot. The meat did not stay fresh. Soon they were hungry again.

30

One day they found a big turtle.

"What a fine meal that will make!" said Hennepin.

But the turtle was a snapping turtle. Father Hennepin almost lost a finger!

The canoe moved slowly down the quiet river. Near Lake Pepin the travelers met some of the Indians they knew. The Indians had left camp to go hunting.

"Let's go with them," said Hennepin. "If hunting is good, the Indians will give us food."

So the white men and the Indians hunted together. When the hunt was over, Hennepin was ready to go back to his Indian home. He thought he might never see any white men again.

But just when he had given up hope, five white men came along! Their leader was a man named Daniel du Lhut. He helped Hennepin and his two friends get away from the Indian villages.

A few years later Hennepin went back to France. The people in France liked Hennepin's stories. All the stories were about the Land of the Great Lakes and the Mississippi. Hennepin wrote many of the stories in a book. People still read that book today.

There is a city in Minnesota called Duluth. Some people think Duluth is an Indian name. It is not. Duluth is another way to spell du Lhut. The city is named for the brave man who helped Father Hennepin.

THINGS TO TALK ABOUT

1. Suppose Hennepin were going from Peoria to Mille Lacs today. How might he travel? What towns would he pass? Look at a map while you talk about these things.
2. Why did some Indians put elm bark on their houses? What do we use instead?
3. Why did the Indians have so little food?
4. Father Hennepin met du Lhut in what is now Minnesota. What are some of the reasons du Lhut might have had for being there?

SOMETHING TO DO

Make a little Indian village. You may use paper, clay, soap, or anything else you like to work with.

Try to bring a compass to class. Let the other children see how a compass shows which way is north.

THE MAN WHO KEPT TRYING

Once there was a French boy named Robert La Salle. Robert's father was a rich man. Robert could have stayed at home in France. He could have had fine clothes and a beautiful house. He could have been a rich man, too.

But Robert wanted to go to America. He wanted to find out all about this great new land.

When Robert was twenty-three years old he went to Canada. There he learned the Indian languages. The Indians liked to talk to him. Some of them told him about a great river, running to the south.

"A man must travel along the river for eight moons," they said. "Then he will reach the place where the river meets the sea."

Then and there La Salle made up his mind. Some day he would travel all the way along that mighty river.

First he came from Canada to our Land of the Great Lakes. He found out more about the great river that we call the Mississippi. Marquette and Joliet had been on the Mississippi but had not gone all the way to its mouth. The mouth is on the Gulf of Mexico.

La Salle went to France to get help and money for his river trip. One of the people he brought back to help him was a man called Tonti. Tonti had only one hand, but he could cut trees and shoot and paddle a canoe. He even built a sailing ship. It was named the *Griffon*. This was the first sailing ship on the Great Lakes.

La Salle and Tonti and their men sailed the *Griffon* across Lake

Erie. They saw forests and plum trees on the shore. Sometimes they stopped to pick grapes, or hunt bears, or shoot wild turkeys.

From Lake Erie, the *Griffon* sailed across Lake St. Clair to Lake Huron. There a wild storm came up. The wind tossed the ship from wave to wave, just like a rubber ball. Most of the men said their prayers.

Only the pilot did not pray. He was angry. He scolded La Salle and Tonti.

"Why did you bring me on this trip?" he said. "I am a salt-water sailor! What will people say if I die in a fresh-water lake?"

But the storm ended, and no one died. The *Griffon* sailed on into Lake Michigan to what is now Green Bay, Wisconsin.

La Salle and Tonti wanted to go on from there by land or by

canoe. They sent the *Griffon* back the way she had come, carrying a fine load of furs. The men sailing her were going to trade the furs. They could meet La Salle and Tonti later.

No one knows what happened after that. The good ship was never seen again.

La Salle was sad because he had lost his ship. He was sad because the Indians in this part of the country were not his friends. They often told him things that were not true.

Still La Salle went on. He and his men sailed down the St. Joseph River in canoes. Then they carried the canoes over ice and snow to reach the Kankakee and the Illinois rivers. The men went hunting along the way, but they could find almost nothing. They were tired and hungry.

At last they came to an Indian village, where the city of Peoria now stands. The men wanted to stay there for a long rest, but La Salle did not trust the Indians. He built a strong fort a few miles away. He named the fort *Crevecoeur* because he was so sad. *Crevecoeur* is French for "broken heart."

His troubles were not yet over. More men died. Fort Crevecoeur burned down. Tonti and La Salle lost each other in the wild country. It was a long time before they could find each other again. But La Salle would not give up. He went on alone. He tried again, and failed again, to reach the Mississippi.

Perhaps in France they have a saying like this one of ours: "If at first you don't succeed, try, try again." Perhaps La Salle had learned it there, because he did try again.

That time luck was with him. First, he found Tonti. Then, with the help of some friendly Indians, La Salle and Tonti traveled down the Mississippi. One day in April, 1682, they stood at last at the mouth of the river. La Salle felt the salt sea air blow upon his face. Tonti helped the men put up a cross.

La Salle began to speak. He spoke many words. What they meant was this: "All the land from the mouth of the Ohio to the mouth of the Mississippi now belongs to France."

La Salle thought all his work and trouble were for the king of France. But we know now that his work and bravery helped all Americans. That is why we often find the name "La Salle" in our Land of the Great Lakes today.

THINGS TO TALK ABOUT

1. What are some of the things La Salle would see if he took his river trip today?
2. Have you ever had to "try and try again" before you could do what you wanted to do?
3. How did La Salle's trip down the Mississippi help everyone who lives in America?
4. How many things can you think of that are named after La Salle?

SOMETHING TO DO

Act out a play about La Salle's trip to Green Bay. Remember there were sailors on the ship and Indians along the shores. They must be in the play as well as La Salle and Tonti and the pilot.

PADDLE YOUR OWN CANOE

Have you ever had a ride in a canoe?

Most canoes now are painted pretty colors. Most of them have names painted on them, too. People like to give Indian names to their canoes. The Indian names help us to remember that Indians showed the white men how to use canoes.

Now we use canoes for fun. It is great fun to paddle on a lake or river. But it is not a fast way to get where we want to go. When we are in a hurry we use a car or train or airplane.

It was different in the days of long ago. Then the people who lived in our Land of the Great Lakes walked or used canoes. A canoe to an Indian family was like a car to us. Lakes and rivers were like roads for their canoes.

David and his father had a long talk about canoes one day. David's Uncle Ed had sent him a present. The present was a little birch-bark canoe, about one foot long.

"That is just like an Indian canoe," said Father. "Most Great Lakes Indians used birch-bark canoes."

"What if there was no water where the Indians wanted to go?" asked David.

"They went by canoe as far as they could," his father answered. "Then they hid the canoe and walked the rest of the way. Or else they carried the canoe until they reached another river. The places where they carried their canoes are called portages."

"Bruce moved here from Portage, Wisconsin," said David.

"Yes," said his father. "That is a place where the Indians used to carry their canoes. That is why the town of Portage, Wisconsin, has that name."

"The canoes must have been heavy to carry," said David.

"Not if they were made of birch bark," his father told him. "Great Lakes Indians had a good way of making their canoes. An Indian would choose the biggest birch tree he could find. He would take the bark off carefully and clean the inner side. Then Indian women would sew the long pieces of bark together."

"Is that all?" asked David. "I could make a canoe myself if it is that easy!"

"There was a little more to it, David. While the women sewed, the man did something else. He put cedar branches together in the shape of a canoe. Then the bark was put over the branches and tied on carefully."

"With rope?" David wanted to know.

"They did not have rope like ours," said his father. "They used thin branches from the cedar tree. Sometimes they used thin pieces of dried skin from an animal."

"Was the canoe ready to use then?" asked David.

"No. It still had to be well dried. And there were little holes where the tying had been done. Those holes had to be filled with a sticky juice that comes from pine trees. It is called resin. Resin kept the water out."

"I wish we had a big birch tree," said David, looking out the window. "We could make a canoe."

His father laughed. "I don't think we need one, David. We have a car. And I don't need a canoe for my work as some of the Indians did."

"You mean they paddled to work just as you drive to work?" David giggled at the thought.

"In a way, yes," his father answered. "Most of their work was hunting or fishing. Sometimes they went to their fishing or hunting grounds in canoes. And some of them worked right in their canoes."

"How could they do that?" asked David.

"Some of them lived near the places where wild rice grows," said his father. "Wild rice grows in lakes and rivers. In the early days, the Indians paddled their canoes into the rice fields. They would hold the heads of the rice over the side of the canoe. Then they used a stick to make the rice fall into the canoe. Indians still pick wild rice in some parts of Minnesota."

"Indians were lucky," said David. "They could build canoes for nothing. We had to buy our car."

"Remember," said his father, "that the Indian had to do everything for himself. We do some things for other people. Other people do things for us. Some people make cars or shoes or coats. Others do other things. Then we trade with one another. Life was not that easy for the Indian."

David was still looking at his birch-bark canoe. "Look!" he said. "There are words on the bottom. It says 'Paddle your own canoe.' "

"That's a good old saying," said his father. "Can you tell me what it means?"

David thought about it for a minute. Then he made a guess. "Does it mean I should try to do things without help?"

"In a way, yes," his father said. "We all help one another, of course. But there are some things each of us must do for himself. We should not expect anyone else to do them for us. We must 'paddle our own canoe.' "

"Well!" said David with a big smile. "You said our car takes the place of the Indians' canoe. You will have to teach me to drive the car, so I can paddle my own canoe!"

Then he ran outside to float his canoe in the fish pond.

THINGS TO TALK ABOUT

1. What would be a good name for a canoe?
2. Why was Portage, Wisconsin, a good place for the Indians to cross from river to river? You may look at a map while you talk about this.
3. The Indians had to make everything for themselves. We buy most of the things we use. Which way do you think is better? Why?
4. Can you think of some things that people still make instead of buying?
5. Look up the word *resin*. What are some of the things we use it for?
6. What are some of the things David's father might have had in mind when he said: "We should not expect anyone else to do them for us"?

SOMETHING TO DO

Make a canoe out of heavy paper. Make a paddle, too. Try to find out how to paddle a canoe.

There are a few places in the world where some people still go to work in canoes. Try to find out where those places are. Write a short report. Tell where the places are and why canoes are still used there.

TRAPPERS, TRAILS, AND TRADERS

Life was not easy in the Land of the Great Lakes long ago.

Think of having nothing to eat except what you could find out-doors! If hunting was good, there would be meat to eat. The meat might be bear or deer or buffalo or rabbit. Sometimes there would be fish or birds to cook. In the summer there was wild fruit. The Indians knew where to find wild rice and one kind of corn.

Think of building your own house out of trees or bark or the skins of animals! Think of having nothing to wear except what you could make! Think of having no cloth!

The weather can be very cold in our Land of the Great Lakes. Think of having to build an open fire to get warm!

No, life was not easy here in those days. Yet many brave men left their fine homes to come here. Why did they do it?

They had many reasons. Some came to tell the Indians about the white man's God. Some came to find new land for their king.

But many people came to our Land of the Great Lakes to hunt for beaver!

The beaver's fur is warm and heavy. People in Europe liked warm coats made of beaver fur. They would pay much money for the skins.

They would pay for the skins of other animals, too. Otter and muskrat and fox are other animals that lived near the Great Lakes. People came from across the ocean to get those furs, too. But most of all they wanted beaver skins.

The men who came from France to get furs were called "runners

of the woods." That was because they went through the woods setting traps for animals.

The runners and the Indians were often friends. The runners gave the Indians knives and cloth. The Indians gave the runners beaver furs and deerskins.

The skin of the deer was used to make clothes. The Indians knew how to make the skin dry and soft and clean. Soft shoes and coats could be made from deerskin.

There was very little money in the Land of the Great Lakes in those days. But the runners and the Indians did not need money. They used knives and cloth and skins instead. In other words, they traded.

After a while, some of the runners stopped setting traps.

"Let other people run through the woods," they said. "We will be traders instead of trappers. Other people will bring the furs to us. We will trade for furs."

The trader was like a storekeeper. His store was called a trading post. The trading post was a meeting place, too.

The trappers stayed in the woods all winter. The fur of the animals was very thick in the winter. That was the best time to trap.

When spring came, the trappers had many furs. They carried the furs to the trading post. There they met other trappers who had furs to trade. They visited with one another.

The trader took all the furs. He gave the trappers cloth, guns, knives, and other things from Europe.

People in Europe made better things to work with than were made here in those days. Things to work with are called tools. The Indians had tools, too. But most of their tools were made of stone or wood or pieces of bone. Tools from Europe were made of metal.

Metal is hard. It lasts a long time. It can be made very sharp. A metal knife is much better than a stone knife.

Some of the Indians knew about metal before the white men came. They knew where to find metal in the ground. Sometimes they pounded the metal into different shapes. Sometimes they put it into a fire. When it was very, very hot, the metal would melt. It would look like thick, muddy water. Then the Indians could make it run into a shape they wanted. When the metal cooled, it would keep that shape.

But the Indians could not make good traps or tools from metal. They were glad to trade their furs at the trading post. They were glad to get cloth and food and traps and tools instead.

The trappers and the traders did many things for our Land of the Great Lakes. Often people came to live near a trading post. Then the trading post grew into a town. Prairie du Chien, Wisconsin, was once a trading post. So was Winona, Minnesota. There are many towns that started as trading posts.

The trappers gave us many of our roads. Sometimes a trapper found an easy trail through the woods. He used that same trail all the time. He told other trappers about it.

After a while the trail became a wide path. Then more people used it. Some of them made their homes nearby. They used the path as a wagon road. Today it may be a great highway. There are many highways that were trappers' trails long ago.

We are glad that the trappers and traders came to our Land of the Great Lakes. We are glad that there were beavers here. The beavers brought the traders and the trappers.

Beavers still live in the Land of the Great Lakes. The government helps take care of beavers now. There are laws about killing beavers for their fur.

You may have seen a beaver's house. The beaver builds his house himself. It is made from small branches of trees, put together with mud.

The house is built in water. The doors are under the water. So is the place where the beavers keep their food for the winter. Above the water there is a living room. The beaver babies sleep there, too.

Sometimes the water is not deep enough to cover the doors of the beaver's house. Then the beaver builds a wall, or dam.

W.C. MERRIN

Other beavers help him. They bring tree trunks, branches, mud, and stones.

A beaver can cut down a tree with his teeth. He can make a log float down a river to where he wants it to be.

When the beavers have enough wood, they build their wall in the water. The wall, or dam, holds back part of the water. That makes the water around the beaver's house much deeper. The water gets deep enough to hide the door of the beaver's house. Then other animals cannot find it. They cannot break into the house.

There are many beaver dams in the Land of the Great Lakes. There is even a town called Beaver Dam. It is in Wisconsin.

Men have learned many things from beavers. Beavers were the first builders in the Land of the Great Lakes. In a way, it was the beaver's fur that first helped our Middle West to grow.

THINGS TO TALK ABOUT

1. Name some things we get from the land around us, just as the Indians did. Name some things we get by trading with people in other parts of the country. Name some things we get by trading with people in other countries.

2. The story tells about some animals that used to live in our Land of the Great Lakes. Have you ever seen any of those animals? Where? Where could you find pictures of them?

3. There are no "runners of the woods" today, but women still wear furs. How do we get animal skins now?

4. How did the beaver's fur help our Midwest to grow?

5. How does the government help take care of beavers? Can you think of other animals or birds that the government helps protect?

SOMETHING TO DO

Make up a play about a trading post. Have the play take place in the spring, when the trappers are bringing in their furs.

Draw pictures to show how a trading post looked. Draw pictures to show what the trader had ready to trade for the furs he wanted.

See if you can build a beaver house and a beaver dam.

Find out what laws your state has about trapping beavers. Write a report of what you find.

Men, as well as beavers, build dams. Find out why people need to have dams. Write a report of what you find.

Try to find pictures of some big man-made dams. Make a label for each picture, showing the name of the dam and where it is.

UNDER THREE FLAGS

Long ago the Land of the Great Lakes belonged to France. Men like Marquette and La Salle and Nicolet came here from France. They went to many parts of our land where white men had not been before. They put up French flags.

"From now on," they would say, "this land belongs to France."

Men from England came to America, too. At first, most of them stayed near the Atlantic Ocean. They said, "All this land belongs to England."

After a while the French and the English began to fight with one another. One of the things they were fighting about was the Land of the Great Lakes.

"It belongs to us," said the French. "Our flag flies over it."

"It is our land," said the English. "We will shoot down your flag. The English flag will fly over the Land of the Great Lakes."

The Indians said nothing. But they must have thought to themselves, "It is our land. We were here first!" Some of them tried to fight both the French and the English.

The English did win. Their flag did fly over the Land of the Great Lakes.

But then something else happened.

There were some people in America who did not say, "We are English." They did not say, "We are French." They said, "We are Americans." Those people did not want to live under the English flag. They wanted their own flag. They wanted an American flag.

Those men began to fight against the English. They had to fight Indians, too.

One of these early American fighters was a tall man with red hair and bright blue eyes. His name was George Rogers Clark.

Other men were fighting the English in the eastern part of our country. Clark wanted to drive the English out of the Land of the Great Lakes.

Clark's little army did not look like an army at all. There were only about 200 men. Some had hats. Others had caps with foxtails or squirreltails swinging behind them. Their shirts were made of deerskin. Each man had a rifle and a long knife.

The English had a fort at Kaskaskia, in what is now Illinois. It was on the Kaskaskia River, not far from the Mississippi.

Clark wanted to take the fort by surprise. He knew that the English would be watching the rivers. To fool them, he took his men the last part of the way by land.

For days and days they walked! They walked through woods and marshes. Sometimes they had to cut their way through trees and bushes. There were no trails to follow.

At last they came to open country, but they still had far to go. They walked 120 long, hard miles before they reached Kaskaskia. Then, late one afternoon, they saw the fort below them. They saw the English flag blowing in the wind.

"Tomorrow," said Clark, "there will be a different flag!"

Then he and his men lay down in some tall grass and went to sleep.

A few hours before the break of day they were up again. Quietly, under cover of darkness, they crept down to the small Kaskaskia River. There they found boats. Back and forth they rowed the boats, carrying men across the river. They did not make a sound.

Soon all Clark's men had crossed the river. The English fort was right in front of them.

Ever so softly the men climbed up the hill. They went on tiptoe into the fort yard. A few English soldiers were there, but they had no chance to call for help. The Americans, still without a sound, tied up the English soldiers.

Then Clark whispered orders to his men.

The little town of Kaskaskia lay close to the fort. Clark sent most of his men there. They took their places quietly in the streets and waited for a signal from their leader.

Other men stayed to guard the fort. Clark and two of his captains went to look for the English governor.

They found him fast asleep in his bed, a nightcap on his head.

"Wake up! Wake up!" said one of the captains. He shook the governor's shoulder.

"What? What?" cried the governor. He sat up so fast that the tassel on his nightcap hit him in the eye.

"You are a prisoner," Clark told him. "Kaskaskia is an American fort now."

Then the signal went out to the men waiting in the streets. All together they sent up a great shout of gladness.

"Stay in your houses!" they called to the people who lived there. "You will not be hurt if you don't try to run away."

George Rogers Clark and his deerskin army had beaten the English—and they had done it without firing a shot!

This was not the only time Clark took the English by surprise. The very next year he captured the fort at Vincennes, on the Wabash River.

To get to Vincennes, Clark's little army walked for almost three weeks! They walked through ice and snow. Sometimes they had to swim across ice-cold rivers. They did not have enough to eat. But they reached Vincennes when the English were not expecting them!

Clark's men attacked the English fort. They fired first from one place, then from another. They waved many flags and made a lot of noise. Clark had only 130 men. He wanted the English to think he had ten times that many.

The Americans fired at the fort all that night and all the next day. As the sun went down, the English surrendered.

Once more an English flag came down! Once more Clark's flag went up!

Clark's flag was not the flag of the United States. There was no country called the United States at that time. Our country was not called the United States until after the war with England had ended. Then all the land that Clark had won became part of the United States.

At Vincennes, Indiana, today there is a statue of a man in deerskin clothes. It is a statue of brave George Rogers Clark. Because of him and his brave men, the new United States had land all the way to the Mississippi River.

Because of George Rogers Clark, the flag of the United States could fly over the Land of the Great Lakes!

George Rogers Clark did something else, too, for the country he loved. He had a younger brother, William, with red hair like his own. George taught William how to live in the woods. He taught him how to find a trail or make one. He taught him to love the wild land of North America.

Many years later, President Jefferson wanted some men to cross the country to the Pacific Ocean. He chose his own secretary, Meriwether Lewis, to be one leader of the party. He chose young William Clark to be the other.

All that William had learned from his older brother helped him now. Lewis and young William Clark traveled all the way from St. Louis to the Pacific Ocean. No one had ever made that trip before.

George Rogers Clark carried his country's flag to the Mississippi. By his teaching, he helped his brother carry the flag of the United States all the way across our great nation.

THINGS TO TALK ABOUT

1. The flags of three different countries have flown over the Land of the Great Lakes. What are the names of the three countries? Which flag came first?
2. Talk about some of the reasons why so many people wanted to own the Land of the Great Lakes.
3. How would you tell someone else about the kind of man George Rogers Clark was?

SOMETHING TO DO

Act out a play about George Rogers Clark and his men. You may have the English soldiers and the governor in the play.

Draw a map to show the Mississippi and Kaskaskia rivers. Show where the town of Kaskaskia is. Draw a line to show the Wabash River. Put a mark on the line to show where Vincennes is.

Read a book about Meriwether Lewis and William Clark. Write a short story about them.

THE MAN WHO STARTED OHIO

Eleven men in faded uniforms met together one cold March day at an inn near Boston. A raw spring wind was blowing. Above their heads, as they walked in, the tavern sign banged noisily.

General Rufus Putnam looked up at the sign. "The *Bunch of Grapes*," he said. "That's a good name for the birthplace of the Ohio Company. The good earth of the Ohio Valley will give us grapes some day. To brave men who will work hard, Ohio will give many things. Ohio will become an important part of the United States."

The year was 1786. The war against England had ended. The new United States was at peace. But there was much to do before the new country could grow great.

For one thing, there were soldiers who had not been paid. The United States had very little money. How could the government pay the men who had fought for its freedom?

General Putnam knew the answer. The United States owned land. There were miles and miles of good land from the Atlantic to the Mississippi. Why not pay the soldiers by giving them land?

The men who met him at the *Bunch of Grapes* that day had all been soldiers. They thought this would be a good way to get paid.

They called themselves "The Ohio Company" because the land they wanted was along the Ohio River.

The Ohio Company did not get the land for nothing. They bought it from the government, but it cost very little. Some of it cost as little as nine cents an acre.

An acre of land is almost as big as a football field. Just think of getting that much land for only nine cents!

The Ohio Company sold some of the land to other soldiers. The soldiers could pay for part of the land with money. They could pay for the rest just by living on it. The Ohio Company wanted people to come to live on the Ohio land.

It took a long time to get everything ready. Almost two years went by after that first meeting at the *Bunch of Grapes*. Then twenty-two brave people started out from Boston.

In Pennsylvania, they met twenty-six more people who wanted to go to Ohio. That made forty-eight.

General Putnam looked around at his company of forty-eight. "These are good people to start a new town," he thought. "Some are farmers. Some can build houses. One can make shoes. Another builds boats. Each one can do something."

So far the trip had been by land. Now they could travel on the Ohio River. The whole company helped to build some boats. The largest boat was called the *Mayflower*.

The boats carried the Ohio Company to a place where two rivers meet. There, where the Muskingum River meets the Ohio River, they stopped. There they built the first town in Ohio.

France had helped the Americans win their war against the English. The queen of France at that time was Marie Antoinette. Putnam named the new town Marietta, for the queen of France.

First of all, these new Ohioans had to build a high square fence. It was called a stockade.

A stockade was made of tall posts set close together. Each post was pointed at the top. It would be hard to climb over such a fence.

There were some small buildings inside the stockade. Food and guns were kept inside. If anyone came to hurt the settlers, they could hide inside. They would be safe there.

The people of the Ohio Company built homes and stores. They laid out farms. Little by little, Marietta grew into a city.

Other people started other cities in Ohio. Another city on the Ohio River is Cincinnati. Cincinnati was called "the Queen City of the West."

Cleveland, on Lake Erie, grew rich and large. Columbus, in the middle of the state, is now the busy capital city of Ohio.

Ohio is one of the great states in the Land of the Great Lakes. We are glad that General Putnam started it all on that day so long ago. We are glad that what he said came true. Ohio does have grapes today—as well as coal, oil, steel, rubber and many other things we need.

General Rufus Putnam will always be remembered as the man who started Ohio!

THINGS TO TALK ABOUT

1. Why was General Putnam glad his men could do many things?
2. If you were going to start a town, what kind of place would you choose for it? Why?
3. Why did those first Ohioans need a stockade?
4. The story tells you the name of the capital of Ohio. What are the capitals of other states in our Land of the Great Lakes?
5. General Rufus Putnam and his men named one of their boats the *Mayflower*. What do you know about a ship that had the same name?

SOMETHING TO DO

Write down some of the reasons why the Ohio Company came to our Land of the Great Lakes.

Try to find out how your own family happened to move to the state you live in. Write a very short story about it.

Find Boston on a map of the United States. Try to find out how far Boston is from Marietta, Ohio.

TWO FRIENDS AND TWO FORTS

Who was the first white man to live where Chicago now stands?

Most people think that he was a French trader named Le Mai. For a long time Indians were his only neighbors. One of his first white neighbors was another Frenchman, named Ouilmette.

Then some soldiers came to build a fort at the mouth of the Chicago River. Le Mai and Ouilmette helped them.

When the fort was almost finished, an American fur trader came to the shores of Lake Michigan. His name was John Kinzie. He saw the fort being built.

"Many people like to live near a fort," he said to himself. "Where there are many people, trading is good. I think that I will stay here."

Mr. Kinzie went to see Le Mai. "I would like to buy your house," he said. "I want to bring my family here to live."

"I bought my house from a friend," answered Le Mai with a smile. "I will sell it to you, my friend."

"Good!" said Mr. Kinzie. "I have some things to trade that the Indians will like."

"What do you have, my friend?"

"Shoes," said Mr. Kinzie. "I make shoes." There was a twinkle in his eyes as he said this.

Le Mai roared with laughter. "Our good friends, the Indians, do not need your shoes. They like their own shoes, made of elk skin."

"Maybe they will trade their furs for my silver pins and rings,"

59

said Mr. Kinzie. "I will find something that will please them."

So the Kinzie family came to live in what is now Chicago. The Ouilmette family lived nearby.

John Kinzie knew how to make shoes for his family. He knew how to use tools of all kinds. He made Mr. Le Mai's house into a nice home. The Kinzie family lived there for many years. The Indians were their friends.

Later on, other white families came to live at the mouth of the Chicago River. Not all of them knew how to get along with the Indians. Besides, the Indians did not like to have so many people coming to their hunting grounds.

Then another war started between America and England. Sometimes the English paid the Indians to fight the Americans. There was trouble around the fort on Lake Michigan.

One night the Kinzie children were dancing in front of the fireplace in their kitchen. Mr. Kinzie was playing dance music on his violin. Mrs. Kinzie had gone to visit a sick neighbor.

All of a sudden the door flew open! Mrs. Kinzie almost fell into the room.

"The Indians!" she cried. "Indians are coming to burn down the fort!"

Mr. Kinzie still had many friends among the Indians. One of his friends was named Black Partridge.

Black Partridge tried to keep the other Indians from burning the fort. When he saw that he could not stop them, he helped the Kinzie family get away.

Many men who tried to fight the Indians were killed. One of them was Captain William Wells. Wells Street in Chicago is named for him.

There is a street in Chicago named for Mr. Kinzie, too. But Mr. Kinzie did not get killed.

After a while the war with England ended. There was no one to pay the Indians to fight the Americans any more. Life became quiet once again.

The American government sent men to build another fort. They built it near where the first fort had been. More and more people came to live near the new Fort Dearborn.

One day Ouilmette walked past the house where the Kinzies had lived. He saw smoke curling up from the chimney. He looked inside the door. There was his friend, John Kinzie, getting the fire started.

"My friend!" cried Ouilmette. "You were saved. You have come back!"

"Yes, thank God!" said Mr. Kinzie. "I have come back. My family is with me. This is a good place to live!"

"Oh, yes, my friend," said Ouilmette. "It will grow into a big place, too, now that you are here! I will work for you. Farmers will come here, and storekeepers. Some day there will be big boats on the lake. The boats will carry our lumber and furs and grain to far places."

Ouilmette was right. The second fort was even better known than the first had been. John Kinzie set up many trading posts in other parts of the Land of the Great Lakes. Each post had a string of pack horses. Furs from all the posts were sent to Chicago by pack horse.

In time, Fort Dearborn changed into the great city of Chicago. Those first friends and neighbors did not live long enough to see that happen. They would not have been surprised by it, though.

Long ago John Kinzie had said, "This is a good place to live."

Long ago his friend, Ouilmette, had added, "It will be a big place, too."

THINGS TO TALK ABOUT

1. Why is trading good where there are many people?
2. Can you think of a neighborhood near your home that is getting bigger and bigger, just as Fort Dearborn did? What is making it grow?
3. Mr. Kinzie made shoes for his family. We buy our shoes at a store. How many things can you think of that we buy, but that Mr. Kinzie may have had to make?
4. How many things can you think of that helped Chicago grow into a big city?

SOMETHING TO DO

Wilmette is a lovely place near Chicago, on Lake Michigan. It was named for Ouilmette. Can you think of a place near your home that is named for a great man? Find out all you can about that man. Try to find pictures of him and of his home. Write a very short story about him.

Write down all the things you can think of that help to make our Land of the Great Lakes a good place to live.

Try to find a picture of Fort Dearborn. Make a model fort out of soap or cardboard or modeling clay.

OLD MAN RIVER

Linda and her mother were walking to the store. They had waited a long time for the rain to stop. Now the sun was shining, but the streets were wet.

"Look how the water runs down the walk," said Linda.

"And look how it rushes along the street," said her mother. She held out her hand to help Linda jump across the rushing water.

"Where does all the water go?" asked Linda.

"It runs into rivers. The rivers carry it to the sea."

"I wish I could see a big, big river," said Linda.

"You will see one this summer," her mother told her. "We are going to Minnesota. We will see the Mississippi. The Mississippi is one of the great rivers of the world. It is one of the longest of all rivers, if we count its children."

"Oh, Mother!" cried Linda. "Rivers don't have children, do they?"

Mother laughed. "Well, not really. But little rivers do run into big rivers. See how the water on this sidewalk runs down into the street. Water on all the other sidewalks is doing the same thing. That's why there is such a rush of water in the street."

"Just like a river!" said Linda.

"Like a little river, yes," said her mother. "The water from the street will run into a larger river. That river will find a still bigger river. Maybe it will run into the Mississippi. The Mississippi is one of the biggest rivers of all."

"I know the names of some other rivers," said Linda. "The Illinois River is near here. And once we had a picnic on the Des Plaines River."

"We had another picnic on the Kankakee River," her mother remembered. "The Des Plaines and the Kankakee come together. Those two rivers together make the Illinois."

"The Illinois is quite a long river," said Linda.

"Yes," said Mother. "It goes along for about 270 miles. Then it runs into the Mississippi."

"Now I remember!" said Linda. "Daddy told us about a man named La Salle. La Salle was going to the Mississippi. But first he had to take his canoe along the Kankakee and the Illinois."

"That's right," said Mother. "Rivers were like roads. There were no other roads in those days of long ago."

Linda looked down at the little rivers of rain on the street. She thought it would be fun to give them names. "How did the Mississippi get its name?" she asked her mother.

"Mississippi is an Indian word," her mother answered. "We think it means 'big river.' But the Mississippi has nicknames, too."

"I know one!" said Linda. "Old Man River!"

"It has other nicknames, too," her mother said. "Father of Waters is one. Old Father of Rivers is another."

"Fathers have children," said Linda. "I guess people long ago thought rivers did, too."

"Well, it is a nice way to think of it," said her mother. "The Missouri and the Ohio rivers both run into the Mississippi. People liked to think of them as the Mississippi's children."

"I know the Mississippi ends at the Gulf of Mexico," said Linda. "But where does it start?"

"In the north part of Minnesota," said her mother. "It starts from Lake Itasca. We may go there while we are in Minnesota."

"There are lots of towns along the Mississippi," said Linda. "I saw some of them on the map. It would be fun to live beside a river."

"The towns were started because of the river," said Mother. "People who traveled on the river watched for good places to stop. They liked best to stop where someone was living."

"I guess they liked to bring news," said Linda. "It must have been fun to stop and visit."

"That's true," said Mother. "Besides, the travelers liked to buy and sell and trade things. So did the people along the riverbank. They were always glad to see one another."

"Maybe some of the people from the boats stayed there to live," guessed Linda.

"Some of them did. After a while other people came to live where the boats stopped, too. Soon many people lived there. The boat landing grew into a town."

"Did all those towns get started that way?" asked Linda.

"I don't know about every one of them," said her mother, smiling. "But La Crosse, Wisconsin, was once just a boat landing. So was Dubuque, Iowa. St. Louis, Missouri, grew into a big city. One reason was that St. Louis was on the river. All the boats stopped there."

Linda jumped across a little river in the street. The street rivers were not so wide now. Some of the water had run away. The sidewalks would soon be dry.

"Hurry up, little raindrops!" said Linda. "Hurry home to your father!"

She turned to look at her mother. "That's funny!" she said. "Why is the father of waters called Mississippi? If it's a father, I think we should call it Mr. Sippi!"

Then she ran ahead to open the store door for her mother.

THINGS TO TALK ABOUT

1. Many kinds of boats have traveled on the Mississippi. How many kinds can you think of? What kinds of boats use the Mississippi now?
2. How many miles long do you think the Mississippi is? You may look at a map and a scale of miles while you talk about this.
3. Do you know of anyone besides La Salle who traveled on the Mississippi long ago?
4. How many states does the Mississippi touch? You may look at a map while you talk about this.
5. How does a river help a town get started? How does a river help a town grow into a city?

SOMETHING TO DO

Look at a map of the United States. Choose a city that is on the Mississippi. Find out all you can about that city. Try to find out how old it is and how it first began. Try to find out how it got its name. Find out how many people live there now.

See how many rivers you can find that run into the Mississippi. Make a list of those rivers.

FLATBOAT, AHOY!

A brother and sister held each other's hands as they walked down the street. They were in Pittsburgh for the first time.

Pittsburgh was only a small city then, but to Wayne and Amy it looked very big. They were glad they could hear the rustle of their mother's full skirts as she walked behind them.

"There's so much to see," whispered Amy.

Wayne nodded. He had been trying to count the houses. There were stores, too, and offices and inns.

Mother smiled down at them. "Let's all hope very hard that Father can buy a flatboat," she said.

"All right," said Wayne. Then he added, "Why?"

"We don't want to wait for a flatboat to be built," said Mother. "We would have to stay at an inn while we were waiting. That would cost a lot of money. We need the money we have left."

"That's right," said Wayne. He was the older of the two children. He knew it had cost money to come to Pittsburgh from their old home in New Jersey.

"Are you hoping hard," he asked his sister, "that Father will find a flatboat all built and ready for us?"

Amy nodded her head. She and Wayne had always "hoped hard" for things back home. Often the things they hoped for had come true!

"I hoped very hard that we would come to Pittsburgh, and here we are!" said Amy.

68

Amy and Wayne remembered the day their father had told them the good news.

"What would you think if we packed up everything we own?" he had said as he came in. "We'll put everything in the wagon. Then we will start west!"

It had seemed too good to be true!

But they did not take everything they owned. When they started to pack, Father said, "We won't have room for everything. Think hard, and tell me what you want most to take."

"Molly and Moe!" said Wayne and Amy together. Molly and Moe were their two fine horses.

Father laughed. "Well, that's good!" he said. "We could not get along in new, rough land without horses to help us plow."

After that it was not always so easy to choose what to take and

what to leave behind. Mother made a game of it. She let the children help her choose. Then she made a list:

> Molly and Moe
> warm clothes and bedding
> needles and thread
> flower seeds
> dried beans
> flour
> pans and dishes

Father made a list, too. The first thing he wrote down on his list was

> the Bible.

The children made faces at each other when they saw the next thing on the list. It was

> schoolbooks.

Father's list was a long one. Some of the other things he wrote down were:

> gun
> tools and nails
> vegetable seeds
> the cow
> Molly and Moe

Wayne and Amy laughed because their mother and father both had Moe and Molly on their lists.

"One thing is sure," said Father. "We all know we need Molly and Moe! We need them to pull us and the wagon to Pittsburgh. Then they will get on a flatboat with us. We will all ride down the Ohio River to the Land of the Great Lakes. When we settle there, we will need Molly and Moe to help us work the land."

Amy and Wayne tried to think how big the flatboat would have to be. It would have to carry the whole family, two horses, a cow, and all the things in the wagon!

Inside the wagon, baskets of dishes stood next to kettles and pans. Bags of seeds lay on top of boxes of tools and boxes of books. The bedding was put in last. There was just enough room left for the family to sleep on top of the bedding.

Just before the wagon started, animals were added to the load. A crate of chickens, ducks, and geese was tied on underneath the wagon. The cow, tied to the wagon, followed behind.

Molly and Moe pulled forward. The chickens, ducks, and geese set up a noisy squawking. The cow mooed gently. The trip to the Land of the Great Lakes had begun!

But that had been weeks before. Now the land part of the long trip was over. Amy, Wayne, and their mother and father were in Pittsburgh. They were all in a hurry to push on to the lake country. The children had never traveled by boat before. They could hardly wait to get started. Pittsburgh seemed big and fine, but they wanted to get to their new home.

As they walked along the city street, Wayne looked up at his mother. All of a sudden her face lit up! She looked happier than she had looked all day.

"See!" cried Mother. "There is Father, hurrying to meet us!"

Father always hurried when he had good news. Amy forgot that she had felt a little bit afraid in this big city. She went running to meet him. He reached down and picked her up in his arms.

"We'll be on a flatboat before the day is over!" Father almost shouted his news.

"Oh!" said Mother. "You found one you could buy!"

"Better than that! I ran into the Hawkins family. They bought a flatboat last week. They have been waiting to find another family to go with them. Sid Hawkins says it's better to have three men on a flatboat. We can take turns steering."

Wayne looked up quickly. Did his father mean that he, Wayne, could help steer the boat? But his father went on.

"Sid's boy is twenty now, so we'll get along fine. We will build homes near each other, too. Then when we start farming, I'll help Sid. He can use Molly and Moe, too. That way we can pay for our share of the flatboat."

Wayne tried not to be disappointed. He had hoped he could help with the steering. But Father's news was good news anyway. It would be fun to have another family on the long river trip!

"Mr. and Mrs. Hawkins are already on the boat," said Father. "They are waiting for us right now!"

"Flatboat, ahoy!" said Mother happily. "Let us hurry along!"

THINGS TO TALK ABOUT

1. Wayne's father and Mr. Hawkins were glad to help each other. Can you think of some ways in which friends help each other today?
2. If you were moving to another state, what would you take with you? Why is your list different from Wayne's and Amy's?

SOMETHING TO DO

Find Pittsburgh on the map. Try to find some pictures of Pittsburgh or some other large city as it looked more than a hundred years ago. Find pictures of it as it looks today.

THE FLATBOAT MAKES A LANDING

The flatboat looked very big to Wayne and Amy. It was a large raft made of logs. The logs were held together by crossbeams. Toward the end of the boat there was a cabin. It was as large as the big kitchen at their old home. The cabin was built of thick logs, cut to look like boards.

"I never saw such big logs before," said Wayne.

"What are those little slits in the logs for?" asked Amy.

"If we have to fight Indians, we will shoot through those slits," her father said quietly.

"See how thick the walls of the cabin are," said Wayne. "No arrows or bullets can come through those walls!"

"Will we all sleep in the cabin?" asked Amy.

"We'll take turns," said Father. "It will be too crowded if we are all there at the same time. But you children and Mother and Mrs. Hawkins may rest in there whenever you want to."

Wayne started to say that he was too big to rest in the cabin. He wanted to tell his father that he was big enough to help steer the boat. But he decided not to say anything just then.

The bundles and baskets that might be hurt by rain were put inside the cabin. The others were tied to a fence, or rail, that went all around the flatboat. Everything belonging to the two families was on the boat. They were ready to leave Pittsburgh.

"Not every horse gets a chance to flatboat down the Ohio," Wayne whispered to Moe. Moe was tied near the cabin beside

Molly and the cow. The chickens, ducks, and geese were tied to the rail. All the animals seemed to be glad that the wagon trip was over!

Wayne reached over and patted Molly's neck.

"If Father shouts 'Ohio, here we come!'" he said, "don't be afraid. That just means we are starting for our new home."

With a long pole, Mr. Hawkins pushed the flatboat away from the shore. The trip down the Ohio had begun!

The weeks that followed were happy ones.

"The weather favors us," the grownups said in pleased voices. The sky was blue above the green of the hills. The only clouds were pretty little white ones, like sailboats in the sky.

Everyone on board the flatboat liked to look at the hills and woods they passed day after day. Even Molly and Moe would turn their heads to see the land.

One day there was a soft rain. That day the children and the women, too, played games inside the cabin. Wayne and Amy liked to play "When I went to Pittsburgh, I bought—." The first person "bought" something that began with the letter A. The next person bought something that began with B. Each one in turn had to think of something that began with the next letter of the alphabet.

Once when it was Amy's turn she had to buy something that began with the letter I. Everyone laughed when Amy said, "When I went to Pittsburgh, I bought an inn."

"That's one thing we couldn't carry on a flatboat!" said her brother.

The women kept busy keeping the cabin and decks neat and clean. The children took care of the animals. The men, on clear nights, would keep the flatboat floating until very late.

Everyone took turns fishing. The fresh fish tasted good with their meals of dried beans and hard bread.

"We must stop somewhere soon," said Father one day. "Molly and Moe need a place where they can walk around for a while."

The very next day, as they came around a bend in the river, they saw a settlement. There were two cabins near the riverbank. The people on the flatboat shouted happily. Children and grownups hurried out of the cabins. Then they all waved and shouted to one another.

"Look!" cried Mr. Hawkins. "The river current runs close to the bank here!"

Wayne saw his father look quickly at Mr. Hawkins. It was almost as if the two men had a secret. Then his father whispered, "Do you think we can make it? We don't want to disappoint the women this time."

Mr. Hawkins laughed. "It's the horses that need the exercise," he said.

Then everyone was talking at once! The people on the flatboat shouted questions. The families on shore shouted back their answers.

"Yes, yes!" called the people on shore. "You can tie your flatboat here. Steer it this way! That's enough! Now that way, just a bit! There you have it!"

The men on the flatboat did as they were told. Sure enough, the current carried the flatboat close to shore. As the boat floated beneath the branches of a willow tree, Mr. Hawkins threw a rope. One of the men on shore caught it. He tied it around the trunk of the willow tree.

Now the deck of the flatboat was level with the land. But there was still a wide path of water between the boat and the shore. The

75

men from the settlement laid boards across the water. This made a strong, safe bridge.

"Wayne," said his father. "You lead Molly off. I will follow you with Moe."

Wayne tried not to show it, but he felt proud and pleased. Wayne and Molly were the first ashore.

As soon as the horses were on dry land, Father gave Moe's rope to Wayne. Then he went back to help the others off the boat.

Wayne looked around him. Standing next to him was a boy his own age. The two boys grinned at each other.

"You going as far as the Mississippi?" the shore boy asked.

"I think so," Wayne answered.

"That's fine," said the boy. "We are going that far next year. Maybe I'll see you again."

All the grownups around them were shaking hands. The boys shook hands, too.

"Guess you will stay here just long enough to walk the horses," the boy said to Wayne. "But they can take care of themselves. Come to our cabin. I'll show you some real Indian arrowheads and some skins from animals I trapped myself."

Wayne dropped the ropes he had been holding. He gave Molly and Moe a quick pat each on the neck. Then he ran after his new friend.

Half an hour later the grownups seemed to be ending their talk. Wayne went back to the willow tree. His mother was coming out of one of the cabins with two other women. Amy was dancing in a circle with some other girls. Father and Mr. Hawkins and young Sid Hawkins were laughing with the other men.

But where were Molly and Moe?

Wayne looked all around. He looked out at the flatboat. He could not see the horses anywhere!

Just then his new friend, Tom, came up behind him. "Tom," said Wayne, "where did the horses go?"

Now it was Tom's turn to look all around. "That's funny!" he said. "We left them right here."

"I was supposed to be walking them around," said Wayne, hanging his head.

"I guess they are walking around, all right," said Tom. "We were so glad to see each other, we forgot those horses. Well, come on. We should be able to find them."

That was a funny thing to say! Did Tom mean they might *not* find Molly and Moe? Wayne stumbled as he followed Tom into a grove of trees. He had never felt worse in his whole life!

From the grove of trees they went into thicker woods. Still there was no sign of the horses. Wayne wondered if his father wouldn't be looking for him, too, by this time. How could he face his family? How could he tell them he had lost the horses? Besides, he loved those horses! The whole family loved them!

Tom looked worried, too. He wasn't talking now. He just pushed ahead, looking for Molly and Moe.

"Tom!" said Wayne, all of a sudden. "Are there any apple trees around here?"

"Sure," said Tom. "There's one right behind Mr. Little's cabin."

"Show me the way," said Wayne. "There's nothing Molly likes better than apples right off a tree! Where Molly goes, Moe always goes, too!"

The boys went back the way they had come. They ran through the grove without stopping to speak to anyone.

"Here's the cabin," said Tom.

They went around to the far side. There, under an apple tree, stood Moe and Molly, munching apples. The horses turned and whinnied as Wayne came up to them.

"Well-ll," said Wayne. "Well, let's give them another walk."

Each leading a horse, they walked quietly around the visiting families. They walked up and down with Molly and Moe. The two boys talked and laughed together like old friends.

When they shook hands and said good-by, Tom winked at Wayne. "I'll see you in the Land of the Great Lakes!" he said. "Look after Molly and Moe till I get there!"

THINGS TO TALK ABOUT

1. Wayne's family was going down the Ohio as far as the Mississippi. What town is at that place now?
2. Play a game like "When I went to Pittsburgh, I bought—." Change it to "When I went down the Ohio, I saw—." You may name anything you might see today.
3. Have you ever spent a vacation in a cabin in the woods? In what ways was it like the cabins that Wayne and Amy might have visited. In what ways was it different?

SOMETHING TO DO

Act out "A Day on a Flatboat." Some of the children may "keep house"; others may take turns steering, fishing, or fixing meals; others may take care of the animals. You may have the flat-boat make a landing, too. Some of the children may be the people on shore.

BOY PILOT

The people on the flatboat were in a hurry to get to their new homes. The men kept the flatboat going almost all the time, even late at night. They were getting tired, but they kept going.

Every once in a while they would see a settler's cabin along the riverbank. Then they would talk of the cabins they would be building soon.

When it was easy to do so, they would land and visit with the settlers. Wayne's father called the settlers "our new neighbors." Wayne, of course, never again forgot to keep a close watch on the horses when they went ashore!

Sometimes the flatboat could not stop. Sometimes the river carried the boat right past the settlement. Even then the people called and waved to one another, as though they were the best of friends.

"You men all look so tired," said Mother one morning. "I think Wayne could help you steer. He has been watching carefully since we left Pittsburgh."

Wayne's father turned to look at him. Wayne almost stopped breathing! He hoped his father would see how big he was getting! He wasn't as big as Sid Hawkins yet, of course.

His father thought for a few minutes. Then he said, "Come and try it, Wayne. Watch out for sand bars, and call for help if you need it. The rest of us men can get more sleep if you help steer."

The flatboat was moving slowly. It would move faster when it floated into stronger current. Wayne climbed to the top of the cabin. He ran over to the long oar that was used for steering. It was called the sweep. With its help he would keep the flatboat on the right path down the river.

The wind blew through Wayne's thick hair. The sun shone on his face. He spread his bare toes strongly. The rough wood felt good under his brown feet. At last he was piloting the flatboat!

Wayne kept hearing his father say "the rest of us men." The words made a little song in his mind. He was very happy.

There was work to be done in this new world, and he, Wayne, would do a man's share of it!

THINGS TO TALK ABOUT

1. Do you know why the flatboat could stop at some places and not at others? Talk about the word *current* and what a river current is.
2. Talk about how you felt the first time your mother or father or teacher let you do something you had always wanted to do.
3. How is a flatboat different from a canoe? Why did the early settlers, like Wayne's family, travel by flatboat instead of canoe?

SOMETHING TO DO

You have read three stories about Wayne and Amy. Write another short story about them. Write about the end of their trip and how you think they started their new home.

STEAMBOAT 'ROUND THE BEND

Long, long ago, the rivers were the roads the Indians traveled on. The Indians could easily float or paddle their canoes for miles. They did not carry very many things with them. The canoes were big enough to hold some furs and a little food. Some simple tools for hunting or for keeping house could be carried, too.

Later the Land of the Great Lakes began to grow. White settlers loaded their belongings onto flatboats and floated down the Ohio. Some of the flatboats went on into other rivers of the Great Lakes country. The people they carried started homes and farms and stores and offices. Flatboats helped the Middle West to grow.

But a flatboat could travel only one way. Flatboats could float downstream, but they could not go back the other way. Once the people were settled, the flatboats did not help them move about.

Then, in 1807, a man named Robert Fulton built a boat that could travel either way. It was called a steamboat.

Some of the river steamboats had a wheel on either side. There was an engine for each wheel. These boats were called side-wheelers.

The first steamboat on the Mississippi had a big wheel and an engine near the back. The wheel was called a paddle wheel. It paddled the water in back of the boat, making the boat move ahead. The boat was called a paddle boat.

Most boats had three decks. The engines were on the bottom deck. The deck hands stayed on this deck. They were called roustabouts. They helped to load the boat and to keep it clean. When

the boat was carrying grain or meat or lumber, that was kept on the bottom deck, too.

The middle deck was where the passengers rode. The passengers could walk all around the edge of this deck. On nice days they walked and talked and visited with one another. They could look out and see the beautiful green woods and hills on either side of them.

The cabins where the people slept were on the middle deck, too. So was the big room where they ate their meals or played games.

The top deck was called the texas. The pilothouse was up there. Inside the glassed-in pilothouse, the pilot turned the big steering wheel. He had to be very careful. He had to learn every bend in the river. He had to know where every sand bar was.

Sometimes storms made the river deeper in places. At other places the storms might make the river less deep. The boat might run aground. Driftwood and logs might hurt the river boat. The pilot had to watch out for all these things.

84

Some of the river boats were very beautiful. They were called "floating palaces." Some had pretty rugs, and windows of bright glass in different colors. They had oil paintings and fine velvet curtains. Some even had grand pianos!

They had pretty names, too. One was called *Silver Heels*. Another was *Starlight*. Still another was called *Dew Drop*.

There were many, many steamboats on the rivers of the Middle West. For about a hundred years, the best way to travel was by steamboat. People in the river settlements were always happy when a steamboat came along.

"Steamboat 'round the bend!" someone would cry out. Then

all the people would run down to the landing to see the boat come in. The boats brought things the people in the settlements wanted. They took away things the settlers wanted to sell.

After a while, trains and railroads began to be built. Trains were faster than steamboats. People began to travel by railroad. More and more they shipped their goods by railroad, too. One by one the river boats stopped running.

The few river boats still left are used mostly just for fun. But people have never forgotten how the river boats helped our Land of the Great Lakes grow up!

THINGS TO TALK ABOUT

1. Why could a flatboat travel only downstream? Why could a steamboat travel either upstream or downstream?
2. Why do you think the top deck of a river boat was called the texas? You may look the word up in a dictionary before you talk about this.
3. How did the river boats help the Middle West to grow?

SOMETHING TO DO

Write down as many things as you can think of that the steamboats may have carried to the river settlements. Choose one of all those things. Write a short story about that same thing today. Is it made or raised in your state, or does it have to be brought from somewhere else? If it is shipped into or out of your state, tell how it travels. What is it used for?

THE BATTLE OF TIPPECANOE

"He is here! Tecumseh is here!"

It was a warm summer morning in Vincennes. This little city in Indiana Territory was a busy, quiet place. There had been no fighting with the Indians for many years.

But now the great Indian chief, Tecumseh, had come to Vincennes. His men had made a camp outside the city. There were almost 400 Indians with Tecumseh.

Tecumseh lived near the mouth of the Tippecanoe River. He lived in what is now the north part of Indiana. He and his brother had started an Indian village there. Tecumseh's brother was called "The Prophet." The village was called "Prophet's Town."

Tecumseh was like a father to the other Indians. He wanted them to farm their lands and lead good lives. He wanted them to keep their lands.

William Henry Harrison was governor of Indiana Territory. He was a good man, too, but he wanted the Indians to sell their land. Some of the Indians did give up their land.

When Harrison heard that Tecumseh was in Vincennes, he went to meet the Indian leader.

"I invite you to a meeting in the governor's house," said Harrison.

"No," said Tecumseh. "We will meet together in that grove of trees."

So Governor Harrison had a table and chairs taken out of the house to the grove of trees.

The people of Vincennes wondered what was happening.

"Please take a chair at the table," said Harrison. "It is the wish of your great white father, the President, that you sit at our table."

"The sun is my father!" Tecumseh said. He sat down on the ground.

Then he went on speaking. "You are taking all the lands of the Indians," he said. "You will drive us into the great lakes! You had no right to make a bargain with a few foolish Indians! The land belongs to us! Let us have back what you have taken from us!"

Harrison would not give back the land. He talked to Tecumseh in a friendly way. But nothing he said made Tecumseh feel any better.

Once Tecumseh jumped to his feet. He waved his tomahawk and shouted, "You lie! You lie!"

Tecumseh's men jumped to their feet, too. They waved their tomahawks. Then some of the white soldiers ran up to the governor. They had guns in their hands.

For a little while not a person moved. Tecumseh stood without a word. Then he waved to the Indians to sit down again. He bowed to Harrison and sat down once more.

Not very much was said after that. At last Governor Harrison said that the meeting was over.

The next day Tecumseh came to see Harrison. "I am sorry I spoke when I was angry," he said. "But I spoke the truth."

Tecumseh was very quiet, and he stood very tall. Harrison liked the Indian chief and felt sorry for him. But he would not give up the land.

Tecumseh made a trip to the Mississippi River. He went to ask the Indians there to stand together with all the other Indians. He also thought he might get the English to help him get the land back from the United States.

While Tecumseh was away, his brother was the leader of the Indians. The Prophet sent one of his braves to see the governor.

"The Prophet will meet with you," said the brave. Then he went to get his leader.

But Harrison was afraid of a trick. He was afraid the Indians were getting ready to fight.

"The Prophet and his braves may try to surprise us," he said. "We must surprise them first!"

Harrison was right. The Prophet did send his men to fight. They thought the white men would be getting ready for the meeting.

But the white men were ready with guns. The Indians lost the battle.

If the great Tecumseh had been there, the battle might have turned out differently. If Tecumseh had been there, he and Harrison might have had another meeting. Maybe there would not have been a battle at all.

Because the battle was fought near the Tippecanoe River, it was called the Battle of Tippecanoe. There were brave men fighting on both sides. Both sides were fighting for the Land of the Great Lakes.

THINGS TO TALK ABOUT

1. Not long ago you read a story about the man who took Vincennes from the English. What was that man's name? Can you tell that story in your own words?
2. Why did Harrison want the Indians to give up some of their land?
3. Do you think Tecumseh and his people were fairly treated?

SOMETHING TO DO

Find out everything you can about William Henry Harrison. Read about him in other books. Write a little story about his life. Write about what happened to him long after the Battle of Tippecanoe.

Read in other books about "Indiana Territory." How was it different from the state of Indiana?

Act out the meeting between Harrison and Tecumseh.

The Battle of Tippecanoe took place in 1811. Find out who was our President then. Write a short story about him.

BLACK HAWK

It would be hard to name the best and the bravest of the great Indian chiefs. Many brave Indians lived in the Land of the Great Lakes. Our country is a better country because such men lived here. All of us have had a chance to learn from them.

One of the bravest and the best was Black Hawk. He was a young chief of the Sauk Indians. Black Hawk lived in a village where the Rock River and the Mississippi come together. The village was called Saukenuk. That meant "the village of the Sauks."

There were not many white people living near Saukenuk. Black Hawk and his people made their living by hunting, fishing, and farming. They raised corn and beans and squash. They had good grass for their horses. They caught fish in the Rock River.

With the coming of winter, the Indians hunted or trapped wild animals to get the fur. They hunted buffalo and deer. They trapped beaver and otter and muskrat. They led busy lives. Most of the time they were quite happy.

Then, one day, one of the Sauk Indians did something the white soldiers did not like. They took him prisoner.

When the Indian was taken, four of his friends went to help him.

"Let our brother go," said the young Indian braves to the soldiers. "Let him go, and we will give you the land on the other side of the river."

The white soldiers wanted the land. They let the Indian go. But the land the white men took was not the land the Indian braves were talking about! The white men took the village of Saukenuk!

Black Hawk was very angry. The four Indian braves had no right to give away a village. The white men had no right to take land that did not belong to them.

Black Hawk tried to talk to the white people, but they would not listen.

"Leave your village!" they told him. "It is our village now!"

Black Hawk and his people would not leave, so the white soldiers burned the village!

Now a real war broke out between the white men and the Sauk Indians. It was called the Black Hawk War. The white men got other Indians to help them. At last Black Hawk and his men were forced to give up.

Black Hawk sent one of his men to the soldiers' camp. The man carried a white flag. The flag meant that Black Hawk was ready to stop fighting. But the soldiers would not let him stop. They kept on fighting. They killed many of the followers of Black Hawk—even the women and children.

Black Hawk himself was not killed. When the war was over he was taken to Washington, to see the President. Black Hawk stood, proud and tall, before President Jackson.

"My people were fighting for their land," said Black Hawk.

The President knew that Black Hawk was a brave man. He knew Black Hawk had fought for what he thought was right.

The place where Black Hawk's village stood is now a part of Rock Island, Illinois. Across the river, in Iowa, is the city of Davenport. Davenport is named for one of the white soldiers who thought he was doing right to fight against Black Hawk.

There is a town on the Rock River called Oregon, Illinois. Near that town there is a statue. The statue was made by a great artist. It is a statue of a great chief—Black Hawk.

Proud and tall and strong and brave, the statue of Black Hawk looks down on the Rock River. It looks down on the fine land that Black Hawk tried to save for his people.

THINGS TO TALK ABOUT

1. Have you ever seen a statue of any other great man? Where was it? Why was it put up?
2. Do you know any stories about other brave Indian chiefs? Maybe you can find such a story and then tell it in your own words.
3. You know how the Sauk Indians made their living. What are some of the ways in which the people of Rock Island make a living now?

SOMETHING TO DO

The Black Hawk War ended in 1832. Who was our President then? Make up a play about that President and his meeting with Chief Black Hawk.

Make a poster showing pictures of the different kinds of animals Black Hawk trapped or hunted. Print the name of each animal beside its picture. Put a blue cross beside the picture of each kind of animal that still lives in our Land of the Great Lakes.

Read other books to find out more about life in a Sauk village. Try to find out what kind of games the Sauk children played. Write a short story or draw a picture of a Sauk village.

GROWING UP IN INDIANA

"Wake up, Abe, wake up!"

Sarah Lincoln pulled at the patchwork quilt that covered her little brother.

Seven-year-old Abe kept his eyes shut tight. He held on to the quilt. This was one day Abe did not want to get up. This was moving day for the Lincolns, and Abe did not want to move.

"Now, Abe, you must get up!" said Sarah, trying to sound like their mother. She often tried to sound that way. She was nine!

"This is the day we move to Indiana," Sarah told him in her best grown-up voice. As though Abe didn't know!

Abe loved Kentucky. He loved their log-cabin farm. He even loved the name of it.

"Rock Spring Farm," he said to himself, as he held on to the quilt for dear life. "We'll never have another farm with such a pretty name!"

But keeping his eyes shut would not help matters. He opened one eye and peeked at Sarah.

Sarah had to laugh! Abe looked so funny, with his black hair standing up straight, and only one eye open! The patchwork quilt was under his chin like a great bright-colored beard.

Abe laughed, too. Then he jumped to his feet. The floor was rough under his bare toes. He did not need to dress. He had been sleeping in his clothes.

Running outside, he washed himself in the cold water of the

spring. His father was tying a heavy sack on the back of a black horse. Abe ran to help him.

Then his mother and Sarah came out of the cabin. Mrs. Lincoln carried Abe's quilt over her arm. Sarah held an apple in one hand, a piece of bread in the other. That was to be Abe's breakfast.

Mrs. Lincoln and Sarah rode on one horse. Abe rode on the other. Mr. Lincoln led the horse Abe was riding.

There were tears in Mrs. Lincoln's eyes as she looked back at the empty cabin. She had moved so many times. Each time they had pushed on to a new frontier.

Abe did not look back. He blinked his eyes very fast as he munched his apple. Indiana seemed far, far away.

The trip was long and not much fun. They crossed the Ohio River. At a place called Thompson's Ferry, Mr. Lincoln got a wagon. The horses pulled it slowly along a wagon trail. Abe and Sarah tried to count the kinds of flowers they saw along the way.

The wagon traveled through a thick forest, in what is now the south part of Indiana. There the children tried to name the kinds of trees they saw.

At last Mr. Lincoln pulled the horses to a stop.

"This is Pigeon Creek," he told his family. "This is our new home."

Abe and Sarah looked around. To them, Pigeon Creek looked just like the rest of the forest. There was no cleared land. They would have to go on sleeping in the wagon for a while. It would take time to cut down trees and build a house.

Abe worked hard each day. He cut the small branches from the trees and bushes. That made it easier for his father to chop down the trees.

As soon as some ground was cleared, the man and boy built a half-faced camp. It was not much of a home. It was made of logs, but it had only three walls. One side was open to the weather.

The Lincolns lived in that half-faced camp for almost a year. It was not so bad in the spring and summer. Abe and Sarah thought it was fun to sleep "almost outside." But when the leaves fell from the trees, the wind grew cold. Then winter came. Sometimes snow blew right inside the little camp.

At last their real log cabin was finished. It seemed like a palace after the camp! Its floor was made of dirt, and there was no glass in the windows. But it did have a fireplace.

By the light from that fireplace, when his day's work was done, young Abe learned to read. His mother taught him to read the only book she had. It was the Bible.

Abe's mother did not live long to enjoy the new log cabin. Abe and Sarah and Mr. Lincoln missed her very much. Abe worked hard at his reading. He knew his mother had wanted him to do that. There was no school at Pigeon Creek. He had to read all by himself.

Then two nice things happened to Abe.

First, a neighbor came to live nearby. The neighbor owned some books. He let Abe take them home, one at a time. Each night Abe lay on the dirt floor in front of the fireplace. As long as the fire gave him light, he tried to read the books.

Second, Mr. Lincoln made a trip to Kentucky. When he came back to Pigeon Creek, he had a new wife with him. Her name was Sarah, too. She was kind and good, as the first Mrs. Lincoln had been. She helped Abe to read. She helped him to study and understand the books he carried home so carefully.

One of the books young Abe liked best was *The Life of Washington*. It was about George Washington, the first President of the United States.

Sometimes there was school for a few weeks now in the frontier settlement. But, in his whole life, Abraham Lincoln was able to go to school for just twelve months.

Abe learned to wrestle and to lift very heavy things. He learned how to measure land. He learned how to find the place where one man's land ended and another man's began. He was always kind and honest. He grew up to be wise and great.

All his life Abe Lincoln was glad about two things. He was glad that his first mother taught him how to read. He was glad that his second mother taught him how to study.

THINGS TO TALK ABOUT

1. Do you know someone who has a patchwork quilt? Can you tell your classmates what it looks like? How is it made?
2. What were some of the things Abe Lincoln did to help his father? What are some of the things you do to help your father?
3. What are some of the differences between reading a book and studying it?

SOMETHING TO DO

Make a collection of pictures showing life on the frontier. Perhaps some of the children have been to Disneyland. They may each tell the class some things about "Frontierland" there. All the other children may ask questions about "Frontierland."

Almost everyone liked Abe Lincoln. Wherever he went he made friends. He talked in a slow, quiet way, but what he said was always worth listening to.

When Lincoln was a young man, he moved to Illinois. Illinois was a new state then in our United States. The new state of Illinois needed new laws.

"You'd better help make our laws, Abe Lincoln. You are a man who reads and thinks about things." That is what his neighbors in New Salem, Illinois, said to young Abe Lincoln.

The people of New Salem chose Lincoln to go to Vandalia, Illinois. Vandalia was the capital of the state at that time. There Lincoln worked hard to get good laws for all of Illinois. He helped to get new roads and canals. He knew that roads and canals would help the Illinois farmers. The farmer needed roads and canals on which to ship his wheat and his cows. The farmer had to ship his cows and wheat to places where they could be sold.

Lincoln had been reading law books for a long time. He read all the law books he could find. At last he knew so much about law that he was able to pass a law test. He became a lawyer.

About that time, the capital of Illinois was moved from Vandalia to Springfield. Lincoln moved to Springfield, too. He wanted to be in the city where state laws were being made.

Springfield was a good place for Lincoln to live then. He had found the kind of work he could do best. Springfield was the best

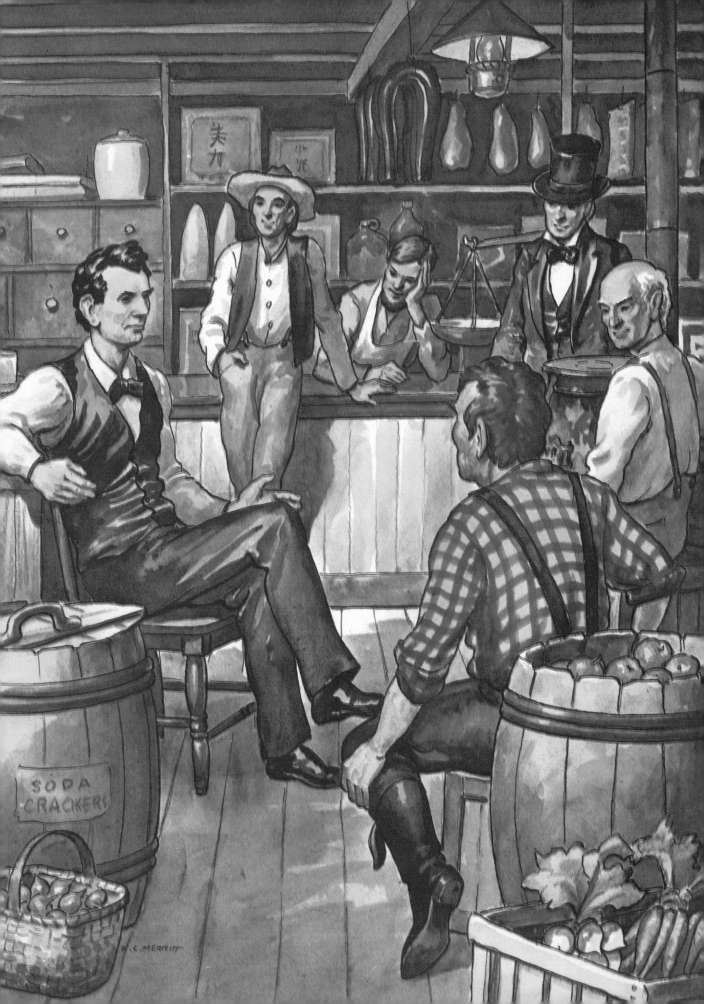

place to do that work. It was in Springfield that he married Mary Todd, a girl from his old state of Kentucky.

Soon everyone in Springfield knew Abe Lincoln. He was the tall, homely man who told such funny stories. He was the kind, gentle man who always helped his neighbors.

The people of Illinois wanted to send a man to Washington, D. C., to speak for them. They sent Abraham Lincoln. Washington was then, as it is now, the capital of the whole nation. There Lincoln helped to make laws for the whole country. In Washington people spoke of Abe as "Lincoln of Illinois."

Later, all the people of the United States wanted to choose a President. The man who was chosen was that same Abe Lincoln.

Abraham Lincoln, the little boy who had been born in a log cabin, became President of the United States. Two different times the people chose him as their President.

Abe lived in the White House in Washington, D. C. But he never forgot the old log cabins. He never forgot the half-faced camp. He never forgot his two gentle mothers who helped him become a gentle man.

Now the whole wide world remembers the gentle man who became our President.

THINGS TO TALK ABOUT

1. Someone may talk about New Salem and how it looks today. Someone else may talk about Springfield, Illinois. A child who has been to Washington, D. C., may tell about that city.

2. Maybe someone in the class knows a lawyer. Talk about the kind of work a lawyer does.
3. How do Americans choose a man to go to Washington to speak for them?

SOMETHING TO DO

There are many, many stories about Abraham Lincoln. Read some of these stories in other books. Write one of these stories in your own words.

The class may choose one or two of the best stories about Lincoln. Act out those stories.

Make up a program for a Lincoln's Birthday party.

THE MIDDLE WEST GROWS UP

A ROAD FOR THE STAGECOACH

There is a town in Ohio called Zanesville. Zanesville got its name from a man who built a road, long, long ago. The man's name was Ebenezer Zane.

Mr. Zane and two other men set out to make a trail. They started at Wheeling, West Virginia and went through Ohio, all the way to Kentucky. As they went along, they marked their trail so that other people could follow it easily.

Their trail had a name. It was called Zane's Trace.

People began to travel along Zane's Trace. Some of them settled along the trail. They began to build homes and stores and blacksmith shops. Mr. Zane himself started the town of Zanesville.

Mr. Zane and some of the other people kept working on Zane's

Trace. They chopped down trees. They cut away bushes. They used horses and oxen to help them pull tree stumps out of the ground. Soon they had made the trail into a road.

The families who were moving to the Land of the Great Lakes in covered wagons used the road. It was very rough and rocky, but it was better than a trail. Sometimes a wagon stuck fast in the mud. The whole family would have to help get the wagon started again. No one seemed to mind. They were glad to have a road to follow to the Land of the Great Lakes.

More and more people came to live in the Land of the Great Lakes. They needed many things that were made in the eastern part of our country. People in the East wanted things from the Middle West. Stagecoaches could carry the things back and forth, but there was no road good enough for a stagecoach to travel on.

Many people sent word to the government in Washington about this. "We want a good road," they said. "A stagecoach must go faster than a covered wagon. We want a road that stagecoaches can travel on all the way to the Great Lakes."

At last the government began to build a road. It was called the Cumberland Road at first, because it began in Cumberland, Maryland. It went from there to Wheeling, West Virginia.

Wheeling was the place where Mr. Zane's road started. After a while the government began to work on Mr. Zane's road, too. It was made part of the Cumberland Road.

The old road grew wider and wider. It was made longer, too. It went as far as Vandalia, Illinois. Later it went all the way to St. Louis. The road belonged to the whole country then, so its name was changed. It was called the National Road.

The National Road would not seem like a good road to us

today. But to those early settlers, more than a hundred years ago, it seemed very wonderful.

Crushed stone covered the mud and filled up the holes. In some places the land was so low that water washed away the stone. Then that part of the road had to be built again. This time it would be built of logs laid close together. A road made of logs was called a corduroy road. A corduroy road was bumpy, of course. But it was dry. It did not wash away.

The English writer, Charles Dickens, once rode along a corduroy road. He did not enjoy the trip! This is what he said about it: "The very slightest jolts with which the carriage fell from log to log seemed enough to break every bone in the human body."

It is true that the new National Road was rough. Stagecoaches could travel on it, though. Everyone in every little town along the way knew when the stagecoach was supposed to get there. Almost everyone came running out to meet it. Sometimes a boy or girl would get a free ride for a little way.

The stagecoaches were painted in bright colors. Some had four horses, some had six. The driver sat outside the coach. Two passengers could sit next to him. Six or more people sat inside.

Bump, bump, bump they went over the rough road. They rode many hours every day, but they never traveled farther than about forty miles. They stopped often to change horses.

Some coaches carried mail and goods as well as people. They left these at places all along the way.

The National Road went through many states. Each state was supposed to take care of its own part of the road.

"The travelers who use the road should pay for it," said the people in those states. They set up toll stations on the road.

When the stagecoach came to a
toll station, it would have to stop.
There would be a long pole across the road, to block it. Each
traveler would have to pay the tollkeeper a certain sum of money.
Then the pole would be raised. The coach could go on. But first,
the driver and his passengers could get out and stretch their legs.
They could buy something to eat at the tollhouse, too. Sometimes
they stayed at a tollhouse overnight.

The National Road was needed because the Land of the Great
Lakes was growing up. The National Road helped it to grow up
even faster.

We still have the National Road today. It looks very different
now. It is wide and smooth and very busy. It is full of cars and
trucks and buses.

The National Road is longer now. It runs all the way across our country. It has a new name, too. We call it Highway 40.

In the Land of the Great Lakes, Highway 40 follows the trail that was once Zane's Trace. It follows the road that had to be built for the bright-colored stagecoaches.

THINGS TO TALK ABOUT

1. What states does Highway 40 pass through now? You may look at a map while you talk about this.
2. A stagecoach traveled about forty miles in a day. How long did it take to go by coach from Zanesville, Ohio, to Vandalia, Illinois? A map and a scale of miles will help you find out.
3. Make believe you are stagecoach passengers. Each one may tell where he comes from and where he is going. Each one may tell why he is making this long, hard trip.
4. Have you ever traveled on one of the toll roads we have today? Which road was it?
5. How are roads built today? Who takes care of them?

SOMETHING TO DO

Make believe you are traveling along the National Road by stagecoach. Choose a place to start and a place to go. Write a short story about one day of the trip. Write down what you see and do along the way.

Now write a short story about that same trip on Highway 40. Tell whether you are going by car or by bus. Tell what you see and do along the way.

JOHNNY APPLESEED

His real name was John Chapman. But early settlers in Ohio and Indiana and Illinois called him "Johnny Appleseed."

Johnny had an apple orchard in Pennsylvania a long, long time ago. Settlers moving west in their covered wagons often stopped at Johnny's place. They bought tiny apple trees, or the seeds for apple trees. Johnny always gave them more than they bought.

The settlers took the trees and seeds to their new homes in the Land of the Great Lakes. Johnny thought about them often. Were the apples growing well in the frontier clearings? Did the young trees get the care they needed?

One day Johnny said to himself, "Why should I stay here and wonder? Why don't I go and find out?"

So he loaded a canoe with bags of apple seeds. He traveled down the Ohio River. Often he stopped to plant an orchard.

Sometimes there were settlers where Johnny stopped. Some of them were settlers who had brought his trees and seeds from Pennsylvania. Johnny helped them take care of their orchards.

Many of the settlers did not have apple trees. "May I plant apples on this bit of land you are not using?" Johnny would ask. If the settler said yes, Johnny would get the ground ready. Then he would plant rows of apple seeds.

Sometimes Johnny stopped just because he saw a place he liked, even if no one lived there. He might clear a piece of land in the middle of a forest. Then he would plant his apple seeds.

At last the seeds he had brought with him were all planted. For the next forty years, until he was an old man, Johnny stayed in the Middle West. He went from orchard to orchard, caring for his trees. When young trees were well started, Johnny would sell some of them to the settlers.

"He gives away more than he sells," the settlers said of him. It was true. His clothes were ragged. He had no home. All he carried with him was a Bible, his seed bag, and sometimes some little trees.

"Poor Johnny Appleseed," people said when they first saw him. But they found out, when they knew him better, that Johnny Appleseed was rich.

He was not rich in money, but he was rich in happiness. He lived in the great outdoors. He read his Bible to all who would listen. He planted trees that make his name remembered even now, more than a hundred years after his death.

Johnny Appleseed was once a hero, too. It was during the War of 1812. In that war, Indians sometimes helped the English to fight against Americans. Johnny found out that Indians were getting ready to attack an American settlement.

Everyone was used to seeing Johnny, trudging along with his Bible and his sack. Neither the Indians nor the English stopped him. He hurried as fast as he could. He traveled thirty miles to the nearest American fort and told the soldiers there what was happening. The soldiers hurried to Mansfield, Ohio, and kept the Indians from attacking.

Johnny was glad that he could help his country in the war. He would be glad and proud if he knew how often his name is heard in the Land of the Great Lakes today.

Next time you see a gnarled and twisted wild apple tree, you, too, may say his name. You, too, may say, "Johnny Appleseed must have walked this way, with his Bible and his bag of seeds."

You, too, may remember Johnny Appleseed, who helped others and who led a happy life in the Land of the Great Lakes.

THINGS TO TALK ABOUT

1. Only a few trees are left of Johnny Appleseed's orchards. Where are there big apple orchards in our Great Lake states today?
2. What other kinds of fruit are grown in the Land of the Great Lakes?
3. Not all early settlers had apple orchards, but most of them had vegetable gardens. What kind of vegetables do you think the settlers raised?
4. Apples have names. How many apple names do you know?

SOMETHING TO DO

Try to find out what kind of care apple trees need. Then write down three things a grower must do to have good apples.

Frontier children often made their own toys. You can make a frontier doll out of a small apple. Cut a face in the apple and let it dry into wrinkles. Stick the apple on a clothespin. Dress the doll in a skirt and shawl. When you have finished, the doll will look like a little old lady of frontier days.

Peel an apple, cut it into thin slices, and hang the slices up to dry. That is how the settlers made their apples last a long time. Make a list called "Ways to Make Food Stay Good for a Long Time." Write down "Drying" as the first way.

BOATS THAT CLIMB STAIRS

When the Land of the Great Lakes was young, Indians traveled on the rivers in canoes. Sometimes they came to waterfalls where canoes could not go safely. Then they picked up the canoe and carried it around the falls. They did the same thing when they wanted to go from one river to another one.

But then the Middle West grew up. People no longer traveled by canoe. They traveled in wagons, stagecoaches, or big boats.

People who had goods to send away liked the boats best. A boat could carry much, much more than a wagon or a stagecoach could. It did not cost so much to send things by boat, either.

The trouble was that a boat could go just so far. No one could pick up a boat loaded with goods and carry it to another river. Besides, people who did not live near a river wanted to send their goods by boat, too.

At last some people in the East *built* a river!

A river that is built by man is called a canal. That first big canal in the East was called the Erie Canal. Boats could travel on the Erie Canal all the way from the Hudson River to Lake Erie. Goods could be shipped by water all the way from Lake Erie to New York City!

"We need canals like that in our Land of the Great Lakes," one Middle Westerner would say to another. "We need canals to the Ohio and the Mississippi rivers. We could use a canal between Lake Superior and Lake Huron."

"And another from Lake Michigan to the Illinois River," his friend would answer. "The more canals we have, the more places we can send our goods by boat. We could ship goods by water to Boston and Baltimore and New Orleans. Those are seaports. From there our goods could go to any country in the world!"

Soon men began to build canals all through the Land of the Great Lakes. They shoveled out long ditches, to make a place where water could flow.

The men who planned the canals were called engineers. Engineers are always looking for ways to build things better. Today our engineers keep building better cars and bridges and dams and roads and airplanes. The canal engineers wanted to build the very best canals. But one thing gave them a lot of trouble at first.

There were many steep hills or waterfalls where canals were being built. The engineers had to find a way to make the boats climb stairs!

They did find a way. Now when a canalboat comes to a steep place, it can climb either up or down!

The "stairs" in a canal are called locks. A lock has big gates at each end. When the gates are closed, no water can get through. When a boat gets to a lock, the first gates open. The boat goes through. Then the gates close behind it.

The gates in front of the boat stay closed. The lock has stone or concrete walls on each side. The boat is "locked in." There is very little water in the lock.

But now some small doors in the walls are opened. More water flows into the place where the canalboat is. The water gets deeper and deeper. The boat goes higher and higher, because it stays on top of the water.

At last the boat is almost as high as the top of the front gates. Then those gates are opened. Beyond them, the water is also high. The water beyond them and the water in the lock flow together. Together they make a level path of water.

The canalboat has "climbed a stair." It is ready to go on through the canal. The gates are left open until most of the water has run out of the lock. Then they are shut until the next boat comes along.

When canals were first built in the Land of the Great Lakes, horses sometimes had to pull the boats along. The path the horses walked along was called a towpath. Tow is another word for pull.

This was a very slow way to travel. Passengers often had to live on the canalboats for days, or even weeks. Sometimes they got tired of riding on the boats. Then they would get off and walk along the towpath for a while.

The English writer, Charles Dickens, once lived on an American canalboat. He wrote a story about it. "We have more than enough food," he wrote. "But the meals are always the same!"

Some people brought their own food. Others waited till the boat stopped at a town. Then they would go to an inn for their meals.

If the boat stopped long enough, the people might sleep at an inn, too. A canalboat cabin was not a very good place to sleep. The beds were not really beds at all. They were narrow boards, covered with thin mattresses. The boards were hung from hooks in the ceiling.

Mr. Dickens did not like to sleep in his canalboat bed. He said it was like sleeping on a bookshelf!

Even though they were very slow, canalboats helped the Land

of the Great Lakes grow up. More and more people came to live in Ohio, Illinois, and Indiana. They raised rich crops of grain and sent the grain to market on canalboats. Their cows grew fat on the good grass of the prairie lands. Beef and cheese brought good prices in markets far away.

Oak and walnut and hickory trees gave the prairie people more lumber than they needed. They had lumber to sell, and they shipped it by canalboat.

Many families who had lived in the East for years began to move west. Many of them moved to the Land of the Great Lakes. Canalboats made moving easier than it had been before.

Every state wanted to grow. Every state wanted more people. People who had already moved to a certain state tried to get others to move there, too.

Of course there was no radio or television in those days of long ago. But there were some songs that were almost like singing commercials. One was about Michigan. This is the way it went:

> "Come all ye Yankee farmers who wish to change your lot,
> Who've spunk enough to travel beyond your native spot,
> And leave behind the village where Pa and Ma do stay,
> Come follow me and settle in Michigania,—
> Yea, yea, yea, in Michigania!"

Canalboats took many people to "Michigania."

The Land of the Great Lakes has many big canals. One of them is the busy Soo Canal, where the ore boats go. Steamboats, too, use the big canals. Some ocean ships can travel all the way from the Great Lakes to the Gulf of Mexico. The Land of the Great Lakes has some of the busiest canals in the whole world.

Hundreds of boats climb stairs in the Land of the Great Lakes each day!

THINGS TO TALK ABOUT

1. How do canals help people who have goods to send away?
2. Can you think of two reasons why more people moved to the Land of the Great Lakes after canals were built?
3. Do you know an engineer? What kind of work does he do?
4. Can you think of other kinds of work done by other engineers?
5. Would you like to become an engineer? Why?
6. You have read how a canalboat climbs up "stairs." Can you tell how a boat going the other way would climb down the same "stairs"?
7. Have you ever seen a canal lock? Have you ever seen a picture of a canal lock? Where was it? How did it look?

SOMETHING TO DO

Make a cardboard model of the kind of bed Mr. Dickens slept in on the canalboat. Use a different piece of cardboard for the ceiling. Make the bed hang from the ceiling.

Draw a row of pictures showing a canalboat as it comes to a lock, goes into the lock, and goes on through the canal.

Try to write a little song or poem about your state, like the one about "Michigania."

People have traveled from east to west in our country in many different ways. Make a chart showing as many of these ways as you can think of. Find or make a picture for each part of the chart. Your first picture might be of a canoe. Print the word "canoe" under the picture. You may show how people have traveled through the years and how they travel now. Be sure to tell on the chart what each picture is.

A GIANT AND THE GREAT LAKES

There were giant trees in the Middle West in the old days. Strong men called loggers cut down the trees. Then they sawed the tree trunks into logs.

The logs were floated down the rivers to sawmills. There they were cut into lumber to build houses. Some of the lumber was used for houses in our Land of the Great Lakes. Most of it was sent away. It was sent by boat through the canals, across the lakes, and down the rivers. Some of it was sent across the oceans.

Everything seemed big in those days. The forests were big. The trees were big. The Great Lakes themselves were big.

No live man was big enough to be the hero of this big new land. So the loggers made one up!

No one knows just how or where or when it happened. Maybe the weather had been bad for a long time. Maybe six or seven loggers were trying to keep warm around their bunkhouse stove.

"I remember one day it got so cold a pot of boiling tea froze solid," one logger may have said. He stood close to the stove and rubbed his cold hands together.

"I remember that, too," called out another, from his bunk. He had crawled into the bunk to keep warm. "Boiling tea froze solid. The ice it made was hotter than that stove!"

"That must have been the year we had two winters, both at the same time." This was a third man speaking, adding to the joke.

Then a fourth man spoke up. "That must have been pretty

bad, all right. But I lived through something worse! Once, up in Michigan, we had summer, winter, spring, and fall, all at the same time!"

"Yes," chimed in another. "One logger up there got sunstroke and froze his feet at the same time. Besides that, he had a bad case of spring fever!"

"He must have been a big, strong man to live through that," the first speaker may have said. "He must have been as big and strong as Paul Bunyan. Paul Bunyan was so big he used to use a pine tree for a comb. Pulled up a fresh one every morning, just to comb his beard!"

And so it went. Loggers in the woods of Michigan and Minnesota and Wisconsin invented their own hero. Whenever loggers met around a campfire, they talked about Paul Bunyan. The more they talked, the bigger he grew. The more they talked, the more stories they made up about this giant logger.

One day someone made up a story about a giant ox that helped Paul Bunyan with his work. The ox was a blue ox, with a silky blue coat and big blue eyes. His name was Babe.

Babe was so big, one logger said, that he measured "forty-two ax handles and a barrel of pickles between horns."

The reason Babe was blue, so said another story, was that he had been born in the Winter of the Blue Snow. Maybe both the ox and the snow were blue because loggers liked that color. It made them think of the skies and lakes they loved.

There is a story about Babe and the Great Lakes, too. One night, so the story goes, Babe wouldn't go to sleep at bedtime.

"Maybe you need some work to make you sleepy," said Paul Bunyan. He hitched Babe up to a giant shovel.

The two of them, the man and the ox, went right to work. By breakfast time the next morning, there were the five Great Lakes!

"They were all dug out and shining in the sun, as blue and pretty as you please," said the logger who made up that story.

Paul Bunyan could do many things. But one thing he could never do. He could not put back the great Midwestern forests.

Once a tree has been cut down, many, many years must pass before another can take its place. People found out too late that logging must be done very carefully. If it is not, young trees are killed and wasted. We found out too late that only a certain number and kind of trees should be cut down each year.

Now we know how to take care of trees. Now the government plants trees in place of some of those that were cut down. But it will be many years before we have great forests again. They will never be as great as those in the old days of Paul Bunyan!

THINGS TO TALK ABOUT

1. Look up the word *conservation*. What is meant by "forest conservation"? Why do we need to conserve our trees?
2. Paul Bunyan stories are sometimes called "tall tales." Can you make up a tall tale about the picture on page 120?

SOMETHING TO DO

Make believe your classroom is a bunkhouse in a logging camp. Each "logger" may tell something about Paul Bunyan.

Find out how the government now helps take care of trees. Write a letter to a friend, telling him about it.

WORKING ON THE RAILROAD

"Where can I find some trappers who are heading west?"

The speaker was a boy of eighteen. He looked even younger. He was quite short. His shoulders were narrow. He was blind in one eye.

The man behind the high desk in the steamboat company office looked up from his work.

"Trappers, eh?" he said slowly. "You want to be a trapper, sonny?"

"I want to get to the Pacific Ocean," said the boy. "I thought I'd go along with the next party of trappers to leave here. Your steamboat company ships furs. You must know all the trappers here in St. Paul."

The man nodded. "Bunch of trappers left here a few weeks ago," he said. "Won't be another bunch going for quite a while. What's your name, son?"

"Jim Hill," the boy answered. "I just came from Canada. I want to get to China. Know where I can get a job while I'm waiting?"

"That's just what I was thinking about," said the man. He pulled down the sleeves of his striped shirt and began to put his coat on. "We ship a lot of flour to the East. I need someone to put labels on the flour bags. You can go to work right now."

James J. Hill never did go traveling with the trappers. He never got to China. It was a long time before he saw the Pacific. But he helped the frontier village of St. Paul become a busy city. He helped the Middle West and the whole United States grow up. The boy from Canada became known the world over. He was called "The Empire Builder."

Hill worked hard in that steamboat office in St. Paul. He learned all there was to know about shipping goods by water. He also learned about railroads.

Trains in those days were very different from our trains today. Some of the first trains were pulled by horses! Others had steam engines that looked like big stovepipes. Black smoke puffed out as the train chugged along. Sometimes dirt and cinders blew all over the passengers.

But trains could go where boats could not go. Trains could travel faster than stagecoaches. Trains did not have to stop at night. All night long, sparks flew upward from their engine fires. People asleep in lonely farmhouses would wake to the friendly, far-off whistle of the train.

There were railroad lines all the way from the Atlantic to the Pacific by 1870. But there was no line from the Land of the Great Lakes to the Northwest.

Jim Hill dreamed of a railroad that would go north to Canada. He wanted to build a railroad that would go from St. Paul to the Pacific. He wanted to build a railroad to what is now the state of Washington.

When the first railroads were built in our country, the government helped pay for them. But the government did not want to pay for a railroad to the Northwest. Very few people lived between

Minnesota and the Northwest. Why should there be a railroad there?

But Jim Hill would not give up his dream. He saved and borrowed enough money to take over a small Minnesota railway. He took a pick and shovel and helped his workmen lay more track.

There was a song the workmen sang. Jim Hill sang it with them. Maybe you have heard it.

> "I've been working on the railroad,
>   All the livelong day.
>   I've been working on the railroad,
>   Just to pass the time away."

Jim Hill and his workmen would make the railroad miles longer. Then he would talk about the fine country his railroad went through. He made people want to move there. When enough people lived along the railroad, Mr. Hill made the line still longer.

Many people did move west on Jim Hill's railroad. But not enough to suit Jim Hill. He sent men all the way to Europe to talk to the people there.

Jim Hill's men talked to people in Ireland and Germany and Norway and Sweden. "Come to the United States," they said. "Jim Hill will help you find good land. He will help you with your farming. He will help you build schools and churches."

And so he did. Jim Hill built his railroad first. Afterwards he helped to build the towns. He knew that towns and cities would make his railroad rich.

Jim Hill's railroad went north from St. Paul to Winnipeg, in Canada. Another part of it went west, across the plains. By 1893, his Great Northern line had reached Tacoma, Washington.

Men and women in our Land of the Great Lakes still talk about Jim Hill. In St. Paul, a great library bears his name. A bank he started is still there. Great Northern and Northern Pacific trains whistle through the Middle West and the Northwest.

Most of all Jim Hill is remembered for the people he brought to the Middle West and the Northwest. You yourself may live in the Middle West today because your great-great-grandfather, long ago, heard about "the Hill country."

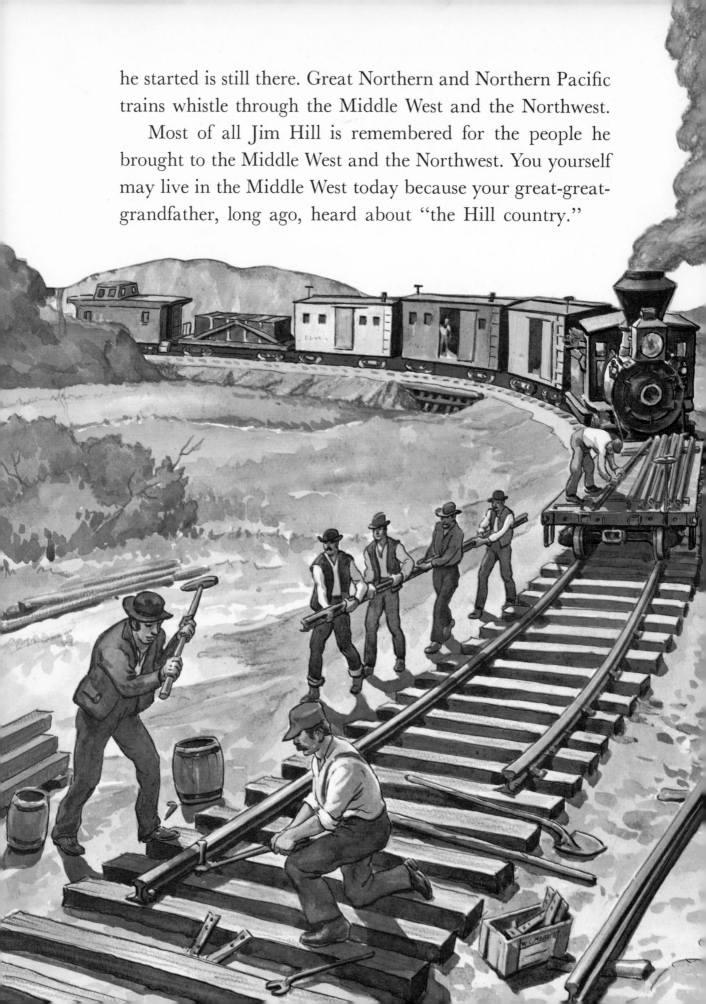

THINGS TO TALK ABOUT

1. Talk about the word *empire*. You may look it up in a dictionary first. Why do you think James J. Hill was called "The Empire Builder"?
2. How did towns and cities help make Jim Hill's railroad rich?
3. Do you know the name of a place where your great-grandfather lived? Can you tell the class something about that place?
4. Have you ever been on a train? Tell about where you slept and where you ate. Tell everything you can remember about the train.

SOMETHING TO DO

On a map of Europe, find Ireland, Germany, Norway, and Sweden. Do you know someone whose great-great-grandfather came from one of those countries? Try to find how out he happened to come to America. Write a very short story about it.

Try to find some pictures of the railroad trains we have today. Write down some of the things that make them different from the trains of long ago.

Make a collection of railroad timetables.

Using a timetable, pick out a place where you would like to go by train. Pick out some places where you would like to stop along the way. Make a list of these places. Show what time your train will get to each place and when you will take a train to the next place. Such a list is called an *itinerary*.

A train has many cars. The cars are used for different things. Write down as many kinds of cars as you can think of. After each one, write what it is used for.

A CITY WITH TWO BIRTHDAYS

The great city of Chicago was first an American fort. Then Mr. Kinzie set up his Chicago trading post. When canals were built, more and more people came to live in the Middle West. As the Middle West grew, so did Chicago.

By 1833, Chicago was a little town.

The prairie farmers sent their grain to Chicago. From Chicago the grain was sent by train or boat to many other places. The farmers sent their cows and pigs to Chicago, too. Chicago stockyards and meat-packing plants became famous all over the world.

Chicago grew fast. By 1837, it was big enough to be called a city! The city of Chicago grew even faster than the little town had grown!

In a way, the city grew too fast. Hundreds of houses and buildings were put up each year. But no one seemed to care how the new buildings looked. No one thought to ask whether a certain kind of building really belonged where it was being built. No one worried about whether or not the buildings were safe buildings.

"Get 'em up! Get 'em up fast! That's all we ask!"

That seemed to be the way the early Chicagoans felt about their buildings.

There was plenty of lumber in the Middle West in those days. A wooden house or building was the easiest, quickest kind to build. Most of the buildings in Chicago were of wood. The big Water Tower was made of stone.

Chicago was a busy city, but it was not like any city we know today. There were no electric lights. There were no telephones. There were no automobiles. Many people raised cows and chickens right in the middle of the city.

One person who owned a cow was Mrs. O'Leary. One October evening in 1871, Mrs. O'Leary was milking her cow. The only light in the barn came from a lantern Mrs. O'Leary had set on the floor.

All of a sudden, the cow kicked over the lantern! The next minute the barn was in flames!

People say that Mrs. O'Leary's cow set the city of Chicago on fire. Maybe that is true. But whether or not the cow was to blame, most of the city did burn down.

For hours and hours the fire raged. A high wind swept the flames from one wooden building to another. Many people ran into Lake Michigan to get away from the fire. At last, after more than twenty-seven hours of horror, rain began to fall. The rain put out the fire, but the heart of the city was in ashes.

One building still stood above the smoking ruins. The Water Tower! Fire had burned out the inside of the building. But the outside, because it was made of stone, had not been harmed. The old stone tower still stands, looking very much as it did before the fire.

The Water Tower taught Chicagoans a lesson.

"Most of our homes and buildings were made of wood," they said. "Once the fire started, the wood fed the flames. Such a thing must never happen here again! We must build a better city. We must build a city of stone and steel. All our buildings must be as strong as the Water Tower!"

Everyone in Chicago began at once to help. As soon as a newspaper could be printed, it was printed with this headline in big letters:

CHICAGO SHALL RISE AGAIN!

Everyone who lived in Chicago wanted that headline to come true!

Neighbor helped neighbor. A man whose store had been burned down stood in the doorway of his home. "Come in," he said to the homeless people on the street. "I have lost my store, but I still have my family and my home. We have extra beds, and a big floor. The kitchen is full of food. My door is open to anyone who needs food or a place to sleep."

People in other cities helped, too. Cincinnati, Ohio, and St. Louis, Missouri, sent trains full of food and clothes. Philadelphia, sometimes called "the city of brotherly love," sent a hundred thousand dollars. Detroit and Boston and many other cities gave Chicago a helping hand.

Even other countries sent help. The great Chicago Library was started with gifts of books from England.

"This is a birthday present for Chicago," said some of the people who sent gifts. "Chicago will be born again. This is a present for the second birthday."

Of course Chicago did rise again. Of course Chicago had a second birthday. And the new Chicago was far better than the old.

The new Chicago is a beautiful city of steel and stone. The first steel skyscraper in the world was built in Chicago.

The new Chicago has laws about the kinds of buildings that can be built. Never again can a fire in one building sweep through the whole heart of the city. There are laws, too, to keep people from starting fires carelessly. And always, since the black days of '71, Chicago has been ready to fight fires. Fire engines, fireboats, fire stations, fire alarms—Chicago's are among the finest.

That is the story of the city with two birthdays. Chicago—a heap of smoking cinders in 1871—is the second largest city in the United States today.

THINGS TO TALK ABOUT

1. What are some of the things each of us can do to keep fires from starting?
2. If a fire did start in your school, what should you do? What should you do if a fire starts in your home?
3. What are some of the things that make buildings safer from fire than they used to be?
4. What does the fire department do to help keep fires from starting? How does the fire department fight fires that have started?
5. Why are there laws against turning in false fire alarms?

SOMETHING TO DO

Each child may write a letter, inviting a fireman to come to school. The class may choose the best letter. Ask the teacher to send it to the fire department. Choose a boy and girl to be host and hostess the day the fireman comes to school.

Make a map of your neighborhood. Show where you live, and where the nearest fire-alarm boxes are. Write in the name of each street shown on your map.

A SCHOOLBOY LONG AGO

Ned Case lay in his bed, half listening to the voices of his mother and father. Then suddenly he was wide awake. His mother had let him sleep late. He might be late for school!

Ned jumped from under his blue and white quilt. As he dressed, he stood near the top of the ladder that led down from his room. He could hear better there.

"I need the boy," Ned's father was saying. "He can do the chores while I get the corn out of the weather."

"Now, Pa," said Ned's mother gently, "it won't snow tonight. This week we can get along without him. It's Ned's turn to make the fire at school and clean up there. He's only nine. That's work enough for him. Besides, this is the day the new teacher is coming here to stay with us."

Ned's father did not answer. Ned knew his father was thinking about the schoolmaster. Mr. Case must be glad, as Ned was, that Mr. Todhunter was coming to their house. But, Ned remembered, his father had not talked about it.

"What will I say to a schoolmaster?" Mr. Case said now. "He will be in my way. He will keep the boy from doing his work around the place."

"Mr. Todhunter is new here," Ned's mother answered. "He'll be wondering what to say to you. And it may be he will teach the boy more than just the school work."

Ned hurried down the ladder. He wanted to help his father with the chores. He wanted to show that he could help at home and go to school, too.

At first Ned had wished that school would never start. But now he could not wait to go to school each day. Would his father keep him at home today? Ned hoped not, but he knew that it might happen. The farm work must come first.

Ned had not said much at home about Mr. Todhunter. Mr. Todhunter was from the East. He had lived in a big city. It seemed to Ned that he knew everything that could be learned from books. But of course Mr. Todhunter could not know much about a farm. Ned hoped his father would try to like Mr. Todhunter anyway.

A bright fire was burning in the fireplace. The warm room felt good after that cold loft where Ned's bed was.

"Good morning, Pa. Good morning, Ma," said Ned. Then he added quickly, "Mr. Todhunter stayed two weeks instead of one at the Wells farm. Mr. Wells said he could have stayed three weeks if he had wanted to. But he is coming here today."

"Well-ll," said Ned's father. His mother said nothing. She was dishing up the breakfast.

Ned sat down on a three-legged stool near the fireplace. His mother handed him a wooden bowl and a wooden spoon. Ned began to eat the steaming porridge. Porridge is something like oatmeal.

Each Friday after school the schoolmaster went to spend a week with a different family. There were no hotels or apartments in this little frontier settlement. There were no rooms to rent.

"I shall start with the first name on the list," Mr. Todhunter had said. "That will be the Brown family. Then I shall go to the last name. That is Wells. After that I shall go back to the beginning of the alphabet again—to Case. Next will come Peterson. And so on."

The schoolmaster had gone back and forth over their names. Now it was time for his visit at the Case cabin.

After breakfast Ned took his slate under his arm. His mother gave him lunch, packed in a basket. Ned kissed her good-by. He looked at his father. He wished he had waked up in time to help with the chores. Mr. Case looked cross.

"Good-by, Pa," said Ned. He ran out the door. Then he ran back in again. He picked a black, burned stick out of the fire. There

were still tiny flames at one end of it. He stamped them out. Then he grinned and held up the stick.

"It's good for doing sums on the big white rock," he said.

When Ned had gone, Mr. Case stood in the doorway looking after him.

"Maybe the boy is right for book learning," said Mr. Case at last.

"Oh, I think he is!" said his wife. "You would have been, too, if you had had a chance to go to school."

The mother and father looked at each other and smiled. They were glad their boy could go to a fine school.

Ned thought it was a fine school, too. He opened the door of the one-room schoolhouse. He was the first one there. The morning was cold, so he made a fire. Then he went outside and brought in enough wood to fill the wood box. The bigger boys had chopped the wood the day before.

Still no one else had come to school. Ned found the broom, made of heavy grasses, and swept around the stove. He swept the school steps, too. Then he took a cloth his mother had given him. He dusted the teacher's desk. He laid his piece of black, burned wood across the desk. When they went outside at lunchtime, the teacher would use that stick. He would use it to write numbers on a big white rock that stood in the schoolyard.

There was another kind of stick in the schoolroom, too. There was a hickory stick standing in one corner. Ned knew what it was for, but Mr. Todhunter had not used it yet.

Now Mr. Todhunter pushed open the door. The three Wells children followed at his heels. Mr. Todhunter smiled and nodded to Ned. Ned felt very grown up.

Soon all the children were at their desks. Then the hours flew by for Ned. Because it was Friday, there was to be a spelldown just before lunch. Ned and James Peterson, sharing a desk, studied their spelling together. The younger children recited their lessons.

At the spelldown, Ned and James Peterson lasted longer than anyone else. Then Ned forgot an "s" in Mississippi. James Peterson was the winner for the week.

At lunchtime all the children sat at the wooden desks to eat. Then they put on their coats and went outside. The boys played "Catch" with a ball the teacher had brought with him from the East. The girls played "Drop the Handkerchief."

When the children were all out of breath they sat on the ground by the white rock. Mr. Todhunter wrote numbers on the rock, like this:

The children called out the answers.

After a while, Mr. Todhunter rang a bell. All the children ran into the school. Then they had a writing lesson.

Ned thought Mr. Todhunter's writing was like the fancy sewing his mother did. Every line was perfect! The schoolmaster had the children copy his writing over and over. Today he wrote:

> If at first you don't succeed,
> try, try again.

Then, because it was Friday, came the part of the week that Ned liked best. Each child had a poem to say. Ned's began like this:

"Those evening bells, those evening bells!
How many a tale their music tells."

When all the poems had been said, the day was over. The children started for their homes. There were no school buses in those days. Some of the children had to walk two or three miles!

Ned felt proud to be walking home with Mr. Todhunter. He felt that he had a friend beside him.

As they walked up the path to the Case cabin, Ned's mother came out to meet them. Where was his father? Wasn't he going to welcome Mr. Todhunter?

Ned looked up at his teacher. Mr. Todhunter was not a big man like Ned's father. He was thin, and he was much younger than Mr. Case. But both were kind and quiet men. Ned hoped everything would be all right.

Then he heard his mother saying, "The Petersons' new calf came early. Mr. Case went over there to help. He has a way with animals, you know. But he should be home for supper."

Mr. Todhunter turned to Ned. "We must help, too," he said.

Ned was too surprised to speak. He didn't know a teacher could do farm work. He thought teachers read books in their spare time. But Mr. Todhunter had his coat off. He was rolling up his sleeves.

"I saw some husked corn in the field over there," the teacher was saying. "I'll start getting it into the shed. We might have snow."

"I'll—I'll help you," said Ned, as soon as he could find his voice.

"Help your mother first," called back the teacher, starting for the field. "Then you can help me. After that we'll milk the cows."

138

Ned's eyes met his mother's. They both smiled. They both knew Mr. Case would like this man. He was a teacher, but he knew what had to be done on a farm!

The boy whistled happily as he followed his mother to the house. He would help her make fresh butter. And while he pumped the handle of the wooden churn, he would say his poem. While his mother listened, he would be saying, loud and clear:

"Those evening bells, those evening bells!
How many a tale their music tells."

THINGS TO TALK ABOUT

1. What were some of the things Ned did to help at school?

   What are some of the things you do to help at your school?
2. What are some of the differences between your school and his?

SOMETHING TO DO

Find a picture of a churn. Try to find out how it works.

Draw or paint a picture of the way you think the Case cabin must have looked. Ned lived there about 1880.

Choose one part of the story about Ned. Act out that part.

Maybe someone in the class knows a person who went to school in a one-room schoolhouse. Ask the teacher to invite that person to come and talk about his schooldays. Choose a boy and girl to be host and hostess the day the speaker comes.

There is an old song called "Schooldays." Try to find that song and learn it. Then write in your own words what you think the words of the song mean.

THE IRON HILL

Far to the north in our Land of the Great Lakes there was once a large hill. The Indians called it the hill of iron. They told many stories about this iron hill. When white men came to Minnesota, the Indians told them the stories.

"Iron!" the white men said to one another. "With iron we can make steel. With steel we can build bridges and ships and schools and railroads. Our country needs a lot of iron."

That was many years ago. The white men began to dig iron from the big hill. Soon there was no hill at all. There was a great big hole instead!

Do you remember the story of Paul Bunyan? Do you remember that people said his pet ox dug five big holes to make our five Great Lakes? That story is a joke, of course. But the story of the iron hill is not a joke.

The men who wanted iron used big shovels to help them dig it out. Each shovel was big enough to pick up a small house. The shovels dug out the iron, and railroad cars carried it away.

The hole that is left is miles wide, miles long, and many, many feet deep. There is still iron in the hole, and men still work to get it out.

The iron hill—or should we say "the iron hole"—is in Minnesota. It is north of Duluth. When iron is taken from the hole, trains carry some of it to the Duluth-Superior harbor on Lake Superior. A harbor is a place where the water is quiet and ships are safe.

The largest harbor on the Great Lakes is the Duluth-Superior harbor. It has long docks that go out over the water. Trains run on the docks. A big boat stops beside each dock and waits there for a train. This boat is called an ore boat.

When iron is first taken out of the ground, people call it "ore." The boat that carries iron is called an ore boat. An ore boat has a smokestack, like a chimney, at one end.

An ore boat may be six hundred feet long. That means it may be twice as long as a football field. Whole trainloads of ore can be dumped into it very fast. Sometimes the big boat is filled in just one hour.

Then the loaded ore boat sails away. It may cross Lake Superior and go through the Soo Canal. It may go into the Straits of Mackinac, and then south to Chicago or to Gary, Indiana. There are many large steel mills in and near Chicago. The mills need ore from the iron hole.

Some of the ore boats cross Lake Huron. From there they go down the Detroit River. They carry ore to mills in Toledo, Ohio; Cleveland, Ohio; Erie, Pennsylvania; or even as far away as Buffalo, New York.

For about seven months each year the ore boats sail from city to city. Then winter comes. The Great Lakes freeze in many places. The ore boats and the men who work on them must wait for spring to come.

When the ice begins to melt, another kind of boat goes out. It is called an icebreaker. An icebreaker is like a snowplow that clears a road for cars. It breaks up the ice on the lakes so the ore boats can sail again.

People who live in the iron country are always glad when the first icebreaker gets through. They smile at each other and shake hands.

"It won't be long now. Spring is almost here," they tell each other.

Ore from the iron hill helped the Middle West grow up. It still helps all of us to have the things we want and need. Bicycles, cars, airplanes, washing machines—even the shiny band around your pencil—may once have been on an ore boat!

THINGS TO TALK ABOUT

1. The story tells about some things that are made from iron. How many more can you think of?
2. How did iron help the Middle West to grow?
3. How is an ore boat different from a flatboat? How is it different from a canoe? Why does the ore boat have to be different?
4. Where do the ore boats take iron ore?

SOMETHING TO DO

Make a map of the Great Lakes. Draw a red line to show how an ore boat might go from Duluth to Chicago, Illinois. Draw a blue line to show how an ore boat might go from Duluth to Buffalo, New York.

There is a picture of an ore boat on the cover of this book. Maybe you can make a little ore boat out of soap.

THE BIG BREADBASKET

Sometimes, in the Land of the Great Lakes, we find something that makes us think of the early days. It might be an Indian arrowhead in a fresh-plowed field. It might be the blade of an old stone ax.

Pipestone, Minnesota, gets its name from a quarry where the Indians got stone for their peace pipes. The quarry is still there.

Many parts of the Middle West still have Indian mounds that were built hundreds of years ago.

The Indians who shot the arrows and mined the stone and built the mounds were farmers. They gathered wild rice and fruit and berries. They planted a few crops. The land gave them all they needed. They did not need very much, of course—just enough to feed themselves.

The first white farmers did not need much more. They cleared away a few trees in the forest. They built cabins and planted little gardens. Some of them planted fruit trees. They raised enough food to feed themselves.

Then steamers and canalboats and wagons and trains began to bring more people. Not all of these people were farmers. The farmers sold food to the newcomers. The boats and trains and wagons carried some of the farmers' crops to markets far away.

Cows grew fat on the waving prairie grass, and were shipped away to market. Wide fields were planted with rich grain. Some of the grain was cut and shipped. Some was made into flour. The round towers of flour mills began to dot the landscape.

The Illinois, Indiana, and Minnesota prairies made fine, flat fields for corn. The trees of Michigan were heavy with cherries, peaches, plums, and apples. Berries grew everywhere in our Land of the Great Lakes.

Wisconsin's rich pasture land helped it to become a dairy state. Wisconsin milk and cheese and butter are known the world over. Ohio raises much food for people and for animals. Fine sheep, horses, hogs, and cows are raised in Ohio.

Our Land of the Great Lakes became a great farming center. Middle Western farmers shipped so much food away that the Lake states got a nickname. "Breadbasket of the World" is what some people call our Land of the Great Lakes.

But while farmers were raising grain and fruit and livestock, other people were doing other things. People who were not farmers came to this rich land.

Some men invented new kinds of farm machinery. Factories were built to make the new machinery. Today, those factories still give work to a great many people. So do the factories where food is canned or frozen before it is shipped away. Chicago has the largest stockyards and meat-packing plants of any city in the world. A great many people work there, too.

Storekeepers and bankers and millers and railroad men all worked with the farmers. All of them helped the Land of the Great Lakes grow up.

Because the Land of the Great Lakes is rich and growing, it has many wonderful things. It has schools and colleges. It has art galleries and museums. It has all the things we need to make life worth living.

Maybe we could say it this way: "The Land of the Great Lakes is a great big breadbasket. It gives the whole world food. It gives us food for our bodies and also for our minds."

THINGS TO TALK ABOUT

1. Have you seen anything in your state that made you think of Indian days? What was it, and where did you see it?
2. What is a landscape? Can you find a picture of a landscape on a postcard or in an old magazine? Can you see a landscape from the window of your room?
3. What is a prairie? Illinois is sometimes called "the Prairie State." Do you know why?
4. What kind of meat do we get from cows? from sheep? from hogs?
5. How does our "Big Breadbasket" give us "food for our minds"?

SOMETHING TO DO

Go to visit a museum. Look for things there that make you think of Indian days. There may be an Indian war bonnet or some Indian tools or clothes. Write a story called "My Visit to the Museum."

Choose one of the states in the Land of the Great Lakes. Try to find out what is raised in that state. Find out what kinds of business it is most famous for. Make a list of its biggest crops. Make another list of its best-known kinds of business.

Make an outline map of your own state. Draw little pictures on the map to show what kinds of vegetables are raised in your state today. Put each picture in a part of the map where that vegetable is raised.

Find out what kinds of animals are raised in your state. Make a chart that shows a picture of each kind of animal, the part of your state in which it is raised, and the kinds of meat we get from it.

NICKNAMES

Mr. Cook was reading the sports page of his evening paper. Linda sat on the arm of his chair, looking over his shoulder.

"Gophers Meet Badgers in Play-off," read Linda out loud. "What does that mean, Daddy?"

David was supposed to be studying his arithmetic, but he looked up at Linda. "It means Minnesota is going to play Wisconsin," he said before his father had a chance to speak. "Anybody but a girl would know that much!"

"Why doesn't the newspaper say 'Minnesota' and 'Wisconsin,' then?" asked Linda. "Why does it say 'Gophers' and 'Badgers'?"

Mr. Cook waited for David to answer, but David seemed to be studying hard.

"Those are nicknames," Mr. Cook told Linda then. "States have nicknames, just as people do."

Linda thought about that for a minute. Then she said, "I know a boy called 'Rusty' Field. I think that's short for 'Russell.' But 'Badger' isn't short for 'Wisconsin'!"

Her father laughed. "I know Rusty Field, too," he said. "He has curly hair, just the color of red rust. Maybe that's how he got his nickname."

"Maybe," said Linda. "But what about Wisconsin?"

David wasn't even looking at his arithmetic now. He was listening.

Father put down his paper. "Badgers are little animals that live under the ground," he said. "A long time ago, Wisconsin had a lot of lead mines. The miners spent so much time underground in the mines that people began to call them badgers. It was just a joke, of course, but the joke lasted longer than the mines did. There is almost no lead in Wisconsin now, but it is still called the Badger State. The teams at the state university are called Badgers."

"What about the Gophers?" asked Linda.

"There are real gophers in Minnesota," said her father. "There are thousands of them now, and there used to be many more. That's why Minnesota is called the Gopher State. University of Minnesota teams are called Gophers."

"At the University of Illinois, the teams are called Illini," said David.

"That's an Indian word," said Father. "It means men, or brave men. But 'Illini' comes from the name of the state. It is not part of a nickname."

"Doesn't Illinois have a nickname?" Linda was going to be very cross if her state didn't have a nickname like the others.

"Illinois has more than one," her father told her. "Its best-known one is 'the Prairie State.' You know why, of course. You have seen some of our rolling prairies."

"Indiana has a funny nickname," said David. "It's 'Hoosier.' What does that mean?"

"Nobody knows for sure," said Father. "One story says the settlers started it. They wouldn't open their cabin doors until they found out who was knocking. They wanted to be sure their visitors were not unfriendly Indians. They used to say, 'Who's here?' If you say 'Who's here?' very fast, it sounds like 'Hoosier.'"

David and Linda both tried it. It sounded so funny they laughed at each other.

"There are two more states in our Land of the Great Lakes," said Father. "Do you know their nicknames?"

"I think Michigan is the Wolverine State," said David, "but I don't know why."

"There are no real wolverines in Michigan now," said his father. "There must have been at one time, though. Indians liked the wolverine's shaggy fur, but people do not wear wolverine now. That's another case where a nickname lasted longer than the reason for it."

"That leaves Ohio," said Linda. "I know a riddle about Ohio. What's round at each end and high in the middle? The answer is O-hi-o."

"But what's its nickname?" asked David.

"That's a riddle Linda can't answer," said their father, smiling. "Ohio is called the Buckeye State. There used to be buckeye trees along the Ohio River. The nut that grows on a buckeye tree has a partly opened shell. Some people think the nut looks like the eye of a deer, or buck. The tree gets its name from the nut. The state got its nickname from the tree."

"Nicknames are fun," said Linda. "I'm going to try to think of one for David."

"Just call me 'Two-Gun,'" said David, going back to his arithmetic.

THINGS TO TALK ABOUT

1. People who live in Chicago are sometimes called Chicagoans. What are people called who live in Minneapolis? in Cleveland? in Detroit? in some other city in the Middle West that you have visited?

2. Do you have a nickname? Do you know how you got it?

3. Do your school teams have nicknames? What are they, and how did the teams get them?

4. Can you think of a city that has a nickname? How did it get that nickname?

5. The United States has a nickname, too. Do you know what it is?

SOMETHING TO DO

Read the sports page of a newspaper. Write down every nickname you find there. Write down the real name that belongs with each nickname.

Even Presidents of the United States sometimes have nicknames. Choose one President who came to be known by his nickname. Write a short story about him. Tell when he was President and how he got his nickname.

YESTERDAY, TODAY, TOMORROW

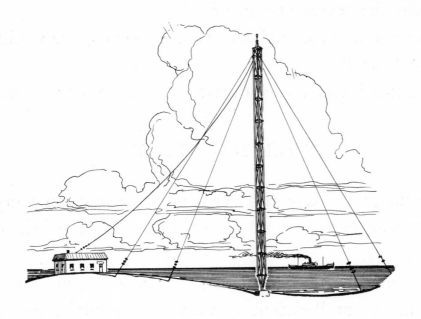

TRAPPERS' TRAIL TO CITY STREET

There is a trappers' trail in the city of Chicago. The other end of the trail is in Vincennes, Indiana.

Indians first used this trail. It was a high piece of ground, easy to walk on. The Indians thought the high ground had once been the shore of a big lake. Maybe they were right. There is no lake at Vincennes now. There has not been a lake in that place for hundreds and hundreds of years.

French and English traders and trappers came to our Land of the Great Lakes. The Indians showed them the same high trail. As more and more people used it, the trail grew longer. It reached all the way from Vincennes, Indiana, to the shore of Lake Michigan. The trail grew wider, too. People began to call it the Vincennes Road.

A fort was built on the Vincennes Road. It was called Fort Dearborn. The settlers who lived south of the fort used the Vincennes Road. They often went to the fort to sell the food they raised on their farms. Those early farmers helped to make the road still better.

Boys and girls and their mothers and fathers still use that road today. Now it is a busy Chicago street called Vincennes Avenue. Old Fort Dearborn grew up. It became the great city of Chicago. The trail of the Indians and the trappers grew up, too. It became a part of the great city.

Many of our crowded highways were once just such trails. Some trails were made by animals. People and animals both like to go places by the easiest way.

You may have seen a path that animals follow to a lake where they go for water. On a farm you might see the path that cows follow to the pasture every day. Maybe you use a path across an empty lot on your way to school. Some day those same paths may be streets or highways.

Highway Number 20 and Highway Number 6 both began a long, long time ago. Trappers kept moving west across our country to find new hunting grounds. Families in covered wagons kept moving west to find new land. They crossed Ohio and Indiana to get to Illinois. Many of them went farther west. The feet of the trappers and the wagons of the farmers made the trails and paths grow wider. Soon they were roads instead of paths.

Later, people began to ride in cars. Cars needed wide, smooth roads. The old roads were made into highways. Many of them followed the same old trails the trappers had once used.

Highway Number 12 to Minneapolis and St. Paul was once a path through wild country. So was Number 66, the highway to St. Louis.

Almost any road or street you walk along may have been a trappers' trail when our Land of the Great Lakes was young. The trails helped our Middle West grow up. Now busy streets and highways help us get the things we want. Highways from every corner of our country lead to where we live.

THINGS TO TALK ABOUT

1. Can you think of a trail or a "short cut" you may have helped to make?
2. How does it happen that many roads today follow the paths of the old trails?
3. How do roads help us get the things we want?

SOMETHING TO DO

Choose a street near your school. Make pictures showing how it must have looked:

     1) when only Indians lived nearby;

     2) when trappers and traders used it;

     3) when it first became a street.

Then make a picture showing how it looks today.

On a road map of the United States, find Highway Number 12. Choose a town that is on that highway. Find out all you can about that town. Try to find out when it was started and how it got its name. Find out how many people live there now. Find out what it is best known for. Write a letter to a friend, telling what you have learned about the town.

Find Chicago on a map. Find Vincennes, Indiana. Use the map scale to find out how far apart they are. How long do you think it must have taken an Indian to walk that long trail? How long does it take to drive from Chicago to Vincennes now? Write down your answers. See whether you and the boy or girl sitting next to you have about the same answers.

Make a list of the kinds of people who have used the Vincennes Road.

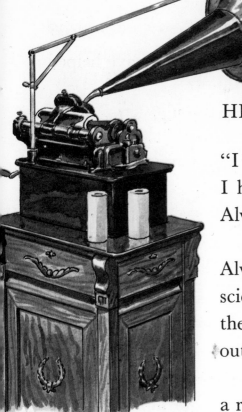

HIS DREAMS CHANGED THE WORLD

"I have so much to do, and life is so short! I have to hurry!" The speaker was Thomas Alva Edison. He was always in a hurry!

Before he was eleven years old, Thomas Alva had read many books on history and science. He had fixed up a laboratory in the basement of his home. There he tried out some of the things he had read in books.

The year that Thomas Alva was twelve, a railroad was built from Port Huron, Michigan, to Detroit. The Edisons lived in Port Huron. Thomas Alva thought it would be fun to work on the train.

At first his mother and father would not let him try to get a job. He won them over.

Then the railroad people would not give him a job. He won them over, too—by saying he would work without pay.

"Just let me ride on the train!" the boy begged. "Let me sell peanuts and popcorn and candy to the passengers."

So Thomas Alva Edison became a "candy butcher." Soon he moved his laboratory to a corner of the baggage car. When he wasn't selling candy or newspapers, he studied or worked in the "lab."

One day Edison saw a three-year-old boy playing on the railroad track. A loose railroad car was rolling toward the child.

The "candy butcher" threw aside his basket! He jumped off his own train and ran to the child. The child's life was saved!

"How can I ever pay you for saving Jimmy's life?" said the child's father. He was the railroad stationmaster at Mount Clemens, Michigan. Part of his job was to use the railroad telegraph.

"I don't want to be paid," Thomas Alva told him. "But I would like to learn telegraphy. Would you teach me?"

So twice a day, when the train stopped at Mount Clemens, Thomas Alva had a lesson in telegraphy. He learned to take code messages faster than almost anyone else. He became a telegrapher.

It was fine to be able to send and get messages. But Edison wanted to find a better way to do it. He dreamed of finding better ways to do almost everything!

The more he dreamed, the harder he worked. The harder he worked, the more things he invented. Edison's inventions changed our way of living. His great dreams changed the world!

Edison helped a man named Bell to build the first telephone. While they were trying to build a good telephone, Edison invented a "talking machine." No one thought it would work—not even Edison. He tried it, though. He turned the crank of the machine and said:

> "Mary had a little lamb.
> Its fleece was white as snow.
> Everywhere that Mary went,
> The lamb was sure to go."

Then he turned the crank to make the machine play back the words.

It worked! The men who were working with Edison could not believe their ears!

"I was a little bit scared myself," said Edison afterwards.

Edison hurried on to his next invention. He found a way to make electric lights. Think how dark the world must have been before Edison made it blaze with electric lights and electric signs!

Even greater, in a way, was Edison's work on the electric motor. Homes and offices and factories today all use electric motors.

The microphone was invented by Edison many years before there were radios. Moving-picture screens and cameras were Edison inventions. Edison built the first electric railways. Edison invented so many things, it is hard to think of all of them!

And what about his first love, the telegraph? He found a way to make one wire carry several messages at the same time. That was what he had dreamed of doing!

Thomas Alva Edison was born in Milan, Ohio. He grew up in Michigan. The Land of the Great Lakes gave him to the world!

The laboratory where Edison worked for many, many years is now in Greenfield Village, near Dearborn, Michigan. It was brought there by Henry Ford, another great Midwesterner.

THINGS TO TALK ABOUT

1. How many things in your school did Edison make possible?
2. If Edison were alive today, what might he be working on?
3. What are some of the things you would like to invent?

SOMETHING TO DO

Learn how to send a message in Morse code.

Try to invent a better way to do something, like cleaning chalkboards.

Read a book about Edison. Make a list of some of his inventions.

THE STORY OF HENRY AND LIZZIE

The story of the United States has been a story of people on the move. The people from Europe who first built homes here built them in the East. Then, little by little, movement toward the West began.

Trappers went westward to find or make new trails. Farmers moved westward to find new rich land. Storekeepers and doctors and teachers and factory owners followed the farmers.

Canoes, flatboats, river steamers, and canalboats carried people and goods by water. Covered wagons, stagecoaches, and trains carried people and goods by land.

But even after the trains came, the people of the United States needed better ways to travel. Many of them lived far from canals or railroad lines. They had to drive their wagons for miles over muddy, bumpy roads to send their goods to market.

Many men dreamed of making land travel better. Many men dreamed of building a wagon or a carriage that would not have to be pulled by horses.

Some of the men who made those dreams come true were born in the Land of the Great Lakes.

One was named Elwood Haynes. He rode over many a bumpy road in Indiana when he was a boy. Charles Duryea was another. His father's farm was near Canton, Illinois. A third man, Ransom Olds, came from Geneva, Ohio.

All those men built cars. But the most famous of all the Great Lakes carbuilders was Henry Ford.

Henry Ford loved watches. He loved to take them apart and put them together again. He loved to fix them.

Henry's family sometimes teased him about his "tinkering," as they called it. If a neighbor had a new watch, Henry's brother or sister might say, "Don't let Henry see it! He will take it apart!"

But when that watch needed to be fixed, the neighbor would remember. He would ask Henry to fix it for him.

One day when Henry was twelve, he and his father took a wagon trip. They went from their home near Dearborn, Michigan, to the city of Detroit. The road was rough and full of holes. The horses pulled and slipped and stumbled. The wagon jolted along.

Suddenly, coming toward them, they saw a steam engine. It

was an ordinary engine, with a boiler. It was used for sawing wood or cutting grain. Henry had seen steam engines before. But this was the first one he had ever seen that could move under its own power! This was the first that did not have to be pulled by horses!

From that day on, Henry knew what he wanted to do. He wanted to build a "horseless carriage."

You know that he succeeded. Ford cars are used in every country in the world. But when he first began to build them, people laughed at him. Almost all wagons and carriages had been made of wood. Henry's cars were made of metal. People began to call them "Tin Lizzies." They made up jokes about "Henry and Lizzie."

Henry didn't mind at all. He remembered the watches.

"The more jokes people make about Fords, the better known Ford cars will be," he said. "I may make up a joke or two myself!"

Soon there were so many Ford jokes that special Ford joke-books were printed. Soon there were so many Ford cars that Henry became one of the richest men in the whole world.

Jokes alone did not make Ford or Ford cars famous. Henry Ford was a man of bold, new ideas. He was not afraid to try new things. He brought about great changes in our whole way of life.

Ford built a car that most people could buy. To keep the cost of his cars low, he had to make many of them at one time. Other cars had been "tailor-made," one at a time. That was expensive.

Ford's factory made thousands of car doors in one place, thousands of headlights in another. There were machines to make every single part of a car. As each part was finished, it was put on a moving belt. The belt carried it to a place where it was joined with another part. The belt was called an assembly line. By the time that door or headlight reached the end of the line, it was part of a whole car!

The assembly line worked so well for Ford that other manufacturers began to use it, too. That meant that other things besides cars could be made more cheaply. It meant that many, many millions of people could afford to buy many wonderful things.

Nowadays, car parts may be made in different cities. Completed cars come off assembly lines in many parts of the United States. But the automobile center of the world is still the state of Michigan. The automobile capital of the world is still Detroit.

Henry Ford is still remembered as Detroit's most famous citizen, and Lizzie belongs to the world.

THINGS TO TALK ABOUT

1. Before there were so many cars, the roads were very poor. Now the United States has the best roads and highways in the world. How do you think this came about?
2. How has farm life changed since the days when there were no cars?
3. How has city life changed since the days when there were no cars?

SOMETHING TO DO

Choose one of the Great Lakes carbuilders. Find out all you can about him. Try to find pictures of the cars he built. Write a short story about him. Illustrate it with pictures of his cars.

Many books and magazine stories have been written about Henry Ford. Read one of them. Then write something about him in your own words.

Visit a factory in your neighborhood and watch an assembly line. Write a short report or draw a picture of it.

THEY DREAMED OF FLYING

"Those Wright boys! They are always up to something!"

That's what the neighbors said about Orville and Wilbur Wright. The boys' father did not mind. He was glad his sons had hobbies. But he made one rule: the boys must earn money to pay for their hobbies.

Orville had many ways to make money after school. He built kites and sold them. He gathered up pieces of old metal and sold them. He even put on a circus!

Wilbur helped his younger brother with some of these things. But Wilbur spent most of his time reading. He liked best of all to read about men who had tried to fly.

The Wright family lived for a time in Richmond, Indiana. When Orville was about twelve, they settled down in Dayton, Ohio. The boys loved Dayton. Their great-great-grandmother had been the first white woman to settle there. Orville and Wilbur were very proud of that.

In Dayton the two boys built a printing press out of an old buggy. When the press was finished, they began to put out a newspaper. They did other printing, too. This was a good business, and they kept it for many years.

Bicycles were coming into fashion about that time. Orville and Wilbur each bought one. Later they started a bicycle shop.

While the Wright brothers worked in their shop, they talked. One thing they loved to talk about was flying. They wished they could build a flying machine!

Orville remembered the kites he had built in his spare time in Richmond. "Let's try to build a kite that will carry a man," he said to his brother. "That might be a good way to start."

The Wright brothers were grown men by that time, but the neighbors still were saying, "Those Wright boys! Always trying something new!"

By 1900 the Wrights had built a kite, or glider, that would carry a man. Then Wilbur wrote to the Weather Bureau.

"Where can we find some flat, open country?" he asked. "It must have sand hills nearby, but not trees or bushes. It should also have plenty of wind. We want to fly a kite."

The Weather Bureau sent the names of six or seven places that might do for kite or glider flying. Wilbur and Orville chose a little place called Kitty Hawk. It was in North Carolina.

Kitty Hawk had a weather station. It had a post office. It had about twenty houses. It had very little else, but it became one of the most famous places in the world. It became famous because Orville and Wilbur Wright went there to fly a kite!

The Wright brothers' dream did not come true the first time they went to Kitty Hawk. They tried their luck in 1900, in 1901, and again in 1902. They did succeed in gliding longer than anyone ever had before. But they had not learned to fly. They did not have a machine that would rise into the air by its own power. Sometimes they were afraid they never would be able to build a real flying machine.

But back they went to their bicycle shop. There they built a wind tunnel. In it they tried out different kinds of wings. They spent every spare minute building models and trying them out. They kept careful notes of everything they learned.

By 1903 the Wrights had a power machine to take to Kitty Hawk. It weighed 750 pounds. It had an engine and a propeller.

December 17, 1903, was a great day. On that day the machine the Wrights had built in their bicycle shop made history. It rose into the air by its own power.

The longest flight that day lasted only fifty-nine seconds. It covered only 852 feet. But it proved that man could fly!

Once more, men of the Land of the Great Lakes had helped to change the world. The Wrights, of Ohio and Indiana, had shown men a way to conquer the sky!

THINGS TO TALK ABOUT

1. How did airplanes help to change the world?
2. What are some ways to earn money after school?
3. What hobbies do you have?
4. Why did the Wrights need open country? sand hills, but no trees or bushes? plenty of wind?
5. In what ways have airplanes changed since December 17, 1903?

SOMETHING TO DO

Collect pictures of early airplanes or early bicycles.

Build a model airplane or a model wind tunnel.

Find out as much as you can about the work of the Weather Bureau. Make a list of some of the things it does for us.

Read a book about the Wright brothers. Write in your own words the story of December 17, 1903, at Kitty Hawk.

HOMES IN THE LAND OF THE GREAT LAKES

Many Indians made houses from animal skins. The first settlers were not much better off than the Indians. They, too, built houses of almost anything they could find on the land. They did as well as they could with the poor tools they had to work with.

Many of the settlers in the Middle West built log cabins. Window glass cost a great deal of money. Most settlers used oiled paper.

There were shutters to keep out the cold. With the shutters closed, the only light came from the fire in the fireplace. There were homemade candles, but they were not often used in the daytime.

Little by little, the settlers built better homes. They began to get better tools. They could get paint, or whitewash. Neat white houses took the place of the log cabins. They had glass windows. They had big stoves as well as fireplaces. Oil lamps and, later, gas lights were used instead of candles.

But even the homes of the very rich were not so comfortable as our homes are today. They were not so well lighted nor so well heated. Few of them had bathrooms. None had electric wiring.

You have read about Edison, the Great Lakes man who gave us electric lighting. His inventions helped make better homes.

There were other Great Lakes men who helped us all have better homes. One of these men was Louis Sullivan. Louis Sullivan was an architect—a person who plans buildings. His office was in Chicago. Mr. Sullivan had a new idea about buildings. He said a building should be built so that the people working in it could work easily. Also, a building should look like the kind of building it is.

One of the men who worked with Sullivan was Frank Lloyd Wright. Mr. Wright was born in Richland Center, Wisconsin. The home he built at Spring Green, Wisconsin, is famous the world over.

Mr. Wright is famous the world over, too.

He believed what Mr. Sullivan said about public buildings. He believed that the same thing was true of homes.

Frank Lloyd Wright built homes and buildings in many countries. Some of the most famous are in the Middle West.

The inventors, architects, and builders, working together, have given us better homes. Because of them we have better light and better heating in our homes. Each one of us has many things at home that early settlers never dreamed of.

But our homes are not through changing. Boys and girls of today will help build even better homes when they grow up.

Some homes now are being built in factories. Pieces are sent to the place where the house is to stand. They are put together there. More such homes may be built in the future.

Other changes are on the way. Some men are looking for better ways of lighting, heating, and cleaning our homes. Others are trying to find ways to make our homes safer.

Homes in the Land of the Great Lakes today look very different from the homes of a hundred years ago. Homes in the year 2000 may look different from the homes of today. Maybe you will help to bring about the changes!

THINGS TO TALK ABOUT

1. Why do we have better homes than the settlers had?
2. What can you do to help make your home a safer place?

SOMETHING TO DO

Draw a plan of a house you would like to live in.

Try to find a picture of a home or building that was planned by Frank Lloyd Wright. Tell whether or not you like it, and why.

RED-BARN-FIVE, TEN-FOR-A-FENCE

David, Linda, and their mother and father were driving to Grandfather's farm. It was a long drive. To help pass the time, David and Linda played a game.

"Red barn, five!" shouted David. He pointed to a red barn on his side of the road.

"Five for me, too!" cried Linda. "There's a red barn on my side, too."

"Ten!" said David a minute later. "There's a fence on my side. That makes fifteen points for me so far."

"I don't care," said Linda. "This is a good side for fences."

But try as she would, she could not find another one. David was having no luck on his side, either.

"Daddy," said Linda at last. "Could we be on the wrong road? I can't find my fences."

"We are on the new cloverleaf road to the new bridge," said her father. "There's the old road down there."

"Oh, yes!" said Linda, leaning over to look out David's window. "We go the other way till we get on the bridge. There's the little stone fence I was waiting for."

"It ought to count on my score," said David. "It's on my side now."

"Why doesn't this road have fences next to it?" asked Linda.

"I guess the farmers along this road have tractors instead of horses," said her father. "Tractors don't need fences."

"There's a kind of fence," said David. "But I can hardly see it."

"It's just one little wire," said Linda, shading her eyes to look. "How can one little wire keep cows out of a cornfield?"

"That wire can," said her father. "It is an electric wire. When the cows touch it, they get an electric shock. The shock isn't strong enough to hurt them, but it makes them stay away from the fence."

"There is a barbed-wire fence," said David. "It is made out of wire that has little sharp points."

"Oh, dear," said Linda. "I'd better find some kind of a fence!"

They had crossed the bridge by now and were going through a town.

"Look, Linda," said her mother. "What do you see between the front yards of the houses?"

"Thick bushes," said Linda. "Why?"

"Could you get through those thick bushes?" asked her mother.

"No-o," decided Linda.

"Then the bushes are really a fence," said her mother. "A fence made of bushes is called a hedge."

"Hurray!" said Linda. "There are three of them right here!"

But there were many hedges on David's side, too, and the children lost count. Then their father signaled for a right turn. He turned the car into a quiet lane and stopped beside a hickory tree. "I want you to see this fence," he said.

Stretching into a field was a long line of overturned tree stumps. The roots on each stump reached up like fingers.

"Is that a fence?" asked David, looking at the long row of stumps.

"Yes," said Father. "A farmer may make a fence out of whatever is handy. If he has stones in his fields, he uses the stones. If he has to clear stumps, he may use them for his fences."

Linda had been quiet for quite a while. When they were on their way again, she said, "I have been thinking."

She said it so solemnly that everyone laughed. But Linda went on. "When we first used to go for drives," she said, "everything was different. There were lots of barns and lots of fences. Now there are whole streets where the barns used to be. There are some fences, but not many of them are around fields. Some of them are hedges in people's yards. A lot of them are walls around factories. And just think! We've seen only two barns all day!"

"You are quite right, Linda," said her father. "Our countryside is changing. It's all a part of growing up, I guess!"

"There's one change I like!" said David, pointing ahead to a brightly painted building. "Let's stop at that new drive-in!"

As his father parked the car, David turned to Linda. "I'll play you Hot-Dog-Five and Ten-for-a-Hamburger," he said.

And they forgot about barns and fences while they read the menu.

THINGS TO TALK ABOUT

1. What kind of "car games" do you play?
2. How many different kinds of fences have you seen?
3. What do you think is causing the countryside to change?

SOMETHING TO DO

Find some pictures of cloverleaf roads. Try to draw a picture or a map of a cloverleaf road you have traveled on. Write down some reasons why more and more cloverleaf roads are being built today.

THE PEACE PIPE HARBOR

Not far from the southern edge of Chicago, there is a lake called Lake Calumet. Calumet is another word for "pipe of peace."

The "peace pipe" lake should become a famous harbor. It was chosen to be an important part of a waterway to the Atlantic Ocean.

Goods from many parts of the West and Middle West can be brought to Calumet Harbor. From there they can be sent by ship all the way to Europe. Ships from Europe can carry goods all the way to Chicago.

For many years ships have sailed from Chicago and other Great Lake ports. They could sail all the way through Lake Ontario. Then they would have to stop. They could not go on to the Atlantic.

When the Indians came to rapids in a river, they carried their canoes past the rapids. But ships are too big to be carried past the rapids in the St. Lawrence River. Here the ships had to stop.

At last, in 1958, a canal, or channel, was built beside the river. The channel is more than a hundred miles long. As the years go by, it will probably be made wider and deeper. Some day even the very largest ships may be able to use the St. Lawrence Seaway.

The St. Lawrence Seaway makes the Land of the Great Lakes a real seacoast. Hides from Middle Western cattle ... powdered milk from Wisconsin farms ... farm machinery ... these are a few of the things that can be sent all the way to Europe by water.

Automobiles can be sent from Detroit to Europe by ship. Steel can be sent from Indiana, rubber from Ohio, wheat from Minnesota.

174

The new seaway will bring more trade to all the Land of the Great Lakes.

The St. Lawrence Seaway belongs to both the United States and Canada. They are peaceful neighbors. It is a happy chance that an important part of their great trade way is called "the Peace Pipe Harbor."

THINGS TO TALK ABOUT

1. How does the new seaway make the Land of the Great Lakes a seacoast?
2. Why is it good to be able to ship goods by water?

SOMETHING TO DO

Make a map to show how a ship might sail from Chicago to a port in England or some other country in Europe.

Find out whether the new seaway will bring changes to your state.

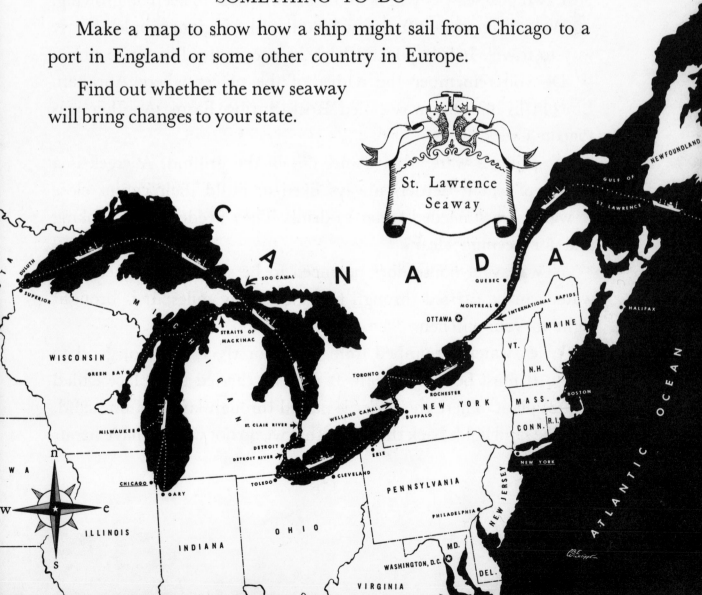

WATER, WATER EVERYWHERE

What is the most precious thing in the whole world?

That is a hard question to answer. One of the most precious things, though, is something you have in your own kitchen! You use it many, many times a day. You use it without thinking about it.

It is water.

Water has always been important to man. Rivers and lakes have always helped new lands grow up. The Great Lakes, the rivers, and, later, the canals helped the Middle West grow up. Now the St. Lawrence Seaway will help the Middle West to keep on growing.

Water is important in a new land because it gives people an easy way to travel. It is important because people need water to drink.

Do you remember the names of the places where Abraham Lincoln lived? One was called Rock Spring Farm. Another was Pigeon Creek.

A spring is water that comes out of the ground. A creek is a stream of water. Settlers always liked to build their cabins close to water. They needed water to drink. They needed it for cooking and for keeping clean.

Nowadays a house does not need to be so near to water. The water can be carried through pipes for many miles. It is brought right to your kitchen.

When water is pumped from a lake or river, it is not good to drink. It must be made clean. It may be carried to a place called a filter plant. There the water is passed through layers of fine sand.

The sand holds back the things that we do not want to have in our

drinking water. Sometimes chemicals are added. They make the water even cleaner. The water that reaches your kitchen is good to drink. Water has other uses, too. Water puts out fires. The water that comes out of fire hydrants does not have to be very clean. It does not have to go through a filter plant. Pipes carry it from the lake or river to the fire hydrants.

Even a long time ago, people knew how to put water to work. Have you ever heard the song called "Down by the Old Millstream"? Mill wheels were turned by the push of falling water. The millstream had to be swift enough to turn a wheel.

When water is heated, it turns to steam. You know that steam has power. You may have watched it lift the lid of a teakettle. People learned how to turn water into steam and put the steam to work. Steam makes engines run.

But there is an even better way that water works for all of us. Water makes electricity.

A powerhouse is built where there is rushing water. The push of the falling water turns big machines in the powerhouse. The machines turn the water power into electric power. The electric power is carried by electric wires to farms and factories and homes.

Electricity lights our homes and streets. It runs all kinds of machinery. With water power, we can have many factories.

There is plenty of water in the Land of the Great Lakes. There are many lakes and rivers. There is almost always enough rain.

In the Middle West, seeds are planted in the spring. Summer rains water them. Farmers do not have to carry water to the fields.

In many parts of our country this is not so. The land dries out in the summertime. Water has to be brought to the field through pipes or ditches. Often it must be brought from many, many miles away.

Many big fields out west must be watered as a lawn is watered. How would you like to water a lawn of several hundred acres every day?

The Land of the Great Lakes is lucky in its wealth of water. It almost always has enough for all its needs.

This wealth of water is one reason that so many people started farms in the Land of the Great Lakes. It is one reason why the Land of the Great Lakes has been called "the Breadbasket of the World."

Wealth of water is one reason why the Land of the Great Lakes is both rich and beautiful!

THINGS TO TALK ABOUT

1. Why is it important to have good water to drink?
2. You know that water helps us to keep clean and healthy. You have read how water works for us. What are some of the ways in which water helps us to have fun?
3. Good things, like water, that come to us from nature, are called *natural resources*. The Land of the Great Lakes has many, many natural resources. Can you name some of them?
4. How many things can you name that you could not have in your home or school without water power?

SOMETHING TO DO

Make a water wheel.

Find out as much as you can about the fire hydrants in your town. Are they all alike? Why were they placed where they are? How many are there? Write a report of what you find out.

Make a list of the ways in which water helps to make the Land of the Great Lakes a good place for a vacation.

Each child may write a letter to the water department in your state. Ask what the water department does. Choose the best letter. Ask the teacher to mail it for the class.

YESTERDAY, TODAY, TOMORROW

The Land of the Great Lakes today is the very same land the Indians knew. It has the same earth and the same water. The sky above it is the same sky.

What, then, makes the Land of the Great Lakes today seem so different from what it was long ago?

Many, many people have helped to bring about the changes. Each generation has learned from all the generations that went before. Each generation has added something to our knowledge and our way of life.

You have learned lessons taught long ago by the Indians and the settlers. You have learned from great men of the past in government and industry. You will learn from the scientists and the inventors. When you grow up, you will hand new knowledge on to your children.

Think of the things we have today that the Indians and early settlers never dreamed of. Steamboats and trains, cars and airplanes help us to travel faster and more comfortably. Yet steamboats use the same Great Lakes the Indians knew. Highways and railroads and even airlines still follow many of the trails the Indians used.

Telegraph, telephones, radios, and television help us keep in touch with people all over the world. A businessman in Akron, Ohio, can call a friend in Detroit. He can send a cablegram to a rubber plantation in South America. When he does either one, he is doing what the Ohio Indians did with smoke signals long ago. He is sending a message to someone he cannot see!

The settlers learned a little bit from the Indians about sending messages. Other men found out a little more, and passed their knowledge on. Little by little, more men studied ways of sending messages. Little by little, whole industries grew up, just to send different kinds of messages!

The first settlers knew how to make water turn a wheel. Little by little, men found more ways to put water to work for them. Now we cannot think what life would be like without the electricity we get from water power.

Indians and settlers knew how to dry meat and fruit to make them stay good to eat. Little by little, through the years, other men have found other ways to make food last a long time. Now we have canned and frozen foods. We have new kinds of dried foods, too. Even soup can be dried out, so that it will last a long, long time.

More than 125 years ago a man in Washington, D. C., gave up his job. He was the head of the office that deals with new inventions.

"I might just as well quit," he said. "Everything has been invented. There cannot possibly be anything more to invent!"

You know how wrong he was! Thomas Alva Edison and the Wright brothers had not even been born yet. Their great inventions had not even been thought of!

There have been great changes since the time of Edison and the Wright brothers, too. In 1942 a whole new age began. It began in the Land of the Great Lakes. It began in a secret place, hidden away under a football field in Chicago. It began when a few men, working in secret, found out how to split the atom. They found out how to put atomic power to work. You, or someone in your class, may carry on the work those men began! One of you may find new ways to use atomic power!

The age we live in has another new, exciting name. It is called "The Age of Space." Settlers long ago kept pushing westward, always to a new frontier. Scientists today and tomorrow will push on to new frontiers, too . . . frontiers of outer space.

Yesterday, today, tomorrow . . . they all seem close together in the Land of the Great Lakes. Each plays an important part in the story of the Land of the Great Lakes. Each plays an important part in the lives of every one of us!

THINGS TO TALK ABOUT

1. Look up the word *generation*. Name some other people who are part of your generation. Name some people of an older generation.
2. The whole business of the newspaper industry is to send messages. What are some of our other "message industries"?
3. A supermarket of today is not itself an invention. Yet inventions made it possible. What are some of those inventions?
4. Why is it important for all of us to study about the past?

SOMETHING TO DO

We need food and clothes and housing, just as the Indians and settlers did. Make a chart that shows (1) some kinds of food, clothes, and housing the Indians had; (2) some kinds the settlers had; and (3) some kinds we have that neither of them had.

Make up three shopping lists. Let the first be of things you might have bought at a trading post. Let the second be one you might take to a market today. Try to think of things for the third list that we do not have today but may be shopping for in years to come.

SOME NAMES AND HOW TO SAY THEM

The marks after each name will help you to say it the right way. They are called diacritical (dī e krit′ i kal) marks. This is what they mean:

′ Say this part of the word a little more strongly than the other parts.
′ Say this part of the word the most strongly.

Say a as in *hat*.   Say i as in *it*.   Say u as in *cup*.
Say ā as in *face*.   Say ī as in *ice*.   Say u̇ as in *full*.
Say ã as in *care*.   Say ü as in *move*.
Say ä as in *father*.   Say o as in *hot*.   Say ū as in *music*.
                            Say ō as in *go*.
Say e as in *let*.   Say ô as in *all*.   Say e as though it were
Say ē as in *be*.   the *a* in *about*.

Akron (ak′ ren)
Arkansas (är′ kan saw)
Atlantic Ocean (at lan′ tik ō′ shen)

Baltimore (bäl′ ti mōr)
Black Hawk (blak hôk)
Black Partridge (blak pär′ trij)
Boston (bos′ ten)
Buckeye (buk′ ī′)
Buffalo (buf′ e lō′)
Bunyan, Paul (bun′ yen, pôl)

California (kal e fôr′ nē e)
Calumet (kal′ ū met′)
Canada (kan′ e de)
Canton (kan′ ten)
Champlain (sham plān′)
Chicago (she kä′ gō)
Chicagoans (she kä′ gō ans)
Cincinnati (sin′ se nat′ i)
Clark, George Rogers (klärk, jôrj roj′ ers)
Cleveland (klē′ vlend)
Columbus (kel um′ bes)
Crevecoeur (krev′ koor)
Cumberland (kum′ ber lend)

Davenport (dav′ en pōrt′)
Dayton (dā′ ten)
Detroit (di troit′)
Dickens, Charles (dik′ ins, chärlz)
Disneyland (diz′ ni land)
Dubuque (de būk′)
du Lhut, Daniel (dü′ lüt′, dan′ yel′)
Duluth (dü lüth′)
Duryea, Charles (dūr′ yā′, chärlz)

Edison, Thomas Alva (ed′ e sen, tom′ es al′ ve)
Erie (ēr′ ē)

Fort Dearborn (fôrt dēr′ bôrn)
Frontierland (frun tēr′ land)
Fulton, Robert (ful′ ten, rob′ ert)

Gary (gãr′ i)
Geneva (je nē′ ve)
Germany (jer′ me ni)
Green Bay (grēn′ bā′)
Greenfield Village (grēn′ fēld vil′ ij)
Griffon (grif′ en)

Harrison, William Henry (har′ e sen)
Haynes, Elwood (hānz, el′ wu̇d)
Hennepin (hen′ e pin)
Hoosier (hü′ zher)
Hudson (hud′ sen)
Huron (hūr′ en)

Illini (il lī′ nī′)
Illinois (il′ e noi′)
Indiana (in′ di an′ e)
Indiana Territory (in′ di an′ e ter′ e tor′ i)
Iowa (ī′ e we)
Ireland (īr′ lend)
Itasca (ī tas′ ke)

Jackson, President (jak′ sen, prez′ i dent)
Jefferson, President (jef′ er sen, prez′ i dent)
Joliet, Louis (jō′ li et′, lü′ wē)

Kankakee (kang′ ke kē′)
Kaskaskia (kas kas′ ki a)
Kentucky (ken tuk′ i)
Kinzie, John (kin′ zē, jon)
Kitty Hawk (kit′ i hôk)

La Crosse (le krôs′)
Le Mai (le mā′)

184

Lewis, Meriwether (lü′ is, mer′ i weth′ er)
Lincoln, Abraham (ling′ ken, ā′ bra ham′)

Mansfield (manz′ fēld)
Marie Antoinette (me rē′ an′ twe net′)
Marietta (mãr′ i et′ e)
Marquette (mär ket′)
Maryland (mer′ e lend)
Mayflower (mā′ flou′ er)
Menomonie (me nom′ ô nē)
Mexico, Gulf of (mek′ se kō′, gulf ov)
Michigan (mish′ e gen)
Midwest (mid′ west′)
Milan (mi lan′)
Mille Lacs (mil′ laks′)
Milwaukee (mil wô′ ki)
Minneapolis (min′ i ap′ e lis)
Minnesota (min′ e sō′ te)
Mississippi (mis′ e sip′ i)
Missouri (mi zůr′ i)
Mount Clemens (mount klem′ enz)
Muncie (mun′ si)
Muskingum (mus king′ gum)

National Road (nash′ en el rōd)
New Jersey (nū jer′ zi)
New Orleans (nū ôr′ li enz)
New Salem (nū sā′ lem)
Nicolet (ni′ kō let)
North America (nôrth e mer′ i ke)
North Carolina (nôrth kar′ e lī′ ne)
Northwest (nôrth′ west′)
Norway (nôr′ wā)

Ohio (ō hī′ ō)
Ohioans (ō hī′ ō ans)
Olds, Ransom (ōlds, ran′ sem)
O'Leary (ō′ lēr′ ē)
Ontario (on tãr′ i ō)
Oregon (ôr′ e gen′)
Ouilmette (wil′ met′)

Pacific Ocean (pe sif′ ik ō′ shen)
Pennsylvania (pen′ sel vā′ ni e)
Peoria (pi ōr′ i e)
Pepin (pep′ in)
Philadelphia (fil′ e del′ fi e)
Pigeon Creek (pij′ in krēk)
Pipestone (pīp′ stōn′)
Pittsburgh (pits′ berg)
Portage (pōr′ tij)
Port Huron (pōrt hūr′ en)
Prairie du Chien (prãr′ i dů shen)

Prairie State (prãr′ i stāt)
Putnam, Rufus (put′ nem, rū′ fus)

Richland Center (rich′ land sen′ ter)
Richmond (rich′ mend)
Rock Island (rok′ ī′ lend)
Rocky Mountains (rok′ i moun′ tens)

St. Anthony (sānt an′ thō nē)
St. Clair (sānt clãr′)
St. Ignace (sānt ig′ nās)
St. Joseph (sānt jō′ zef)
St. Lawrence (sānt lôr′ eṅs)
St. Louis (sānt lü′ is)
St. Paul (sānt pôl′)
San Francisco (san′ fren sis′ kō)
Sauk (sôk)
Saukenuk (sôk′ e nuk′)
Soo Canal (sü ke nal′)
Springfield (spring′ fēld)
Straits of Mackinac (strāts ov mak′ e nô′)
Sullivan, Louis (sul′ e ven, lü′ is)
Superior (se pēr′ i er)
Sweden (swē′ den)

Tacoma (te kō′ me)
Tecumseh (ti kum′ se)
Thompson's Ferry (tomp′ sens fer′ i)
Tippecanoe (tip′ e ke nü′)
Toledo (te lē′ dō)
Tonti (ton′ ti)

Vandalia (van dā′ li e)
Vincennes (vin senz′)

Wabash (wô′ bash)
Washington, George (wosh′ ing ten, jôrj)
West Virginia (west ver jin′ ye)
Weather Bureau (weth′ er būr′ ō)
Wheeling (hwē′ ling)
Wilmette (wil met′)
Winnebago (win′ e bā′ gō)
Winnipeg (win′ e peg)
Winona (wi nō′ ne)
Wisconsin (wis kon′ sen)
Wright, Frank Lloyd (rīt, frangk loid)
Wright, Orville, Wilbur (rīt, ōr′ vil, wil′ ber)

Yankee (yang′ ki)

Zane, Ebenezer (zān, eb′ en ē′ zer)
Zane's Trace (zānz trās)
Zanesville (zānz′ vil)

OTHER BOOKS TO READ

BAILEY, BERNADINE. *Picture Book of Illinois*. Chicago: Albert Whitman and Co., 1957.

———. *Picture Book of Indiana*. Chicago: Albert Whitman and Co., 1950.

———. *Picture Book of Iowa*. Chicago: Albert Whitman and Co., 1952.

———. *Picture Book of Michigan*. Chicago: Albert Whitman and Co., 1958.

———. *Picture Book of Minnesota*. Chicago: Albert Whitman and Co., 1953.

———. *Picture Book of Missouri*. Chicago: Albert Whitman and Co., 1951.

———. *Picture Book of Ohio*. Chicago: Albert Whitman and Co., 1956.

———. *Picture Book of Wisconsin*. Chicago: Albert Whitman and Co., 1957.

BENDICK, JEANNE. *The First Book of Airplanes*. New York: Franklin Watts, Inc., 1952.

BLEEKER, SONIA. *The Chippewa Indians, Rice Gatherers of the Great Lakes*. New York: William Morrow and Co., 1955.

BOTHWELL, JEAN. *The First Book of Roads*. New York: Franklin Watts, Inc., 1955.

BREWSTER, BENJAMIN. *The First Book of Indians*. New York: Franklin Watts, Inc., 1950.

BRINK, CAROL RYRIE. *Caddie Woodlawn*. New York: The Macmillan Co., 1949.

BROCK, EMMA L. *Drusilla*. New York: The Macmillan Co., 1956.

BUCHHEIMER, NAOMI. *Let's Take a Trip to a Fire House*. New York: G. P. Putnam's Sons, 1956.

BUEHR, WALTER. *Through the Locks: Canals Today and Yesterday*. New York: G. P. Putnam's Sons, 1954.

BULLA, CLYDE ROBERT. *Down the Mississippi*. New York: Thomas Y. Crowell Co., 1954.

COFFMAN, R. P. *Famous Explorers for Young People*. New York: Dodd, Mead & Co., 1956.

COMFORT, MILDRED HOUGHTON. *Flatboats and Wagon Wheels*. Chicago: Beckley-Cardy Co., 1948.

COY, HAROLD. *The Real Book about Rivers*. Garden City: Garden City Books, 1953.

CRAWFORD, PHYLLIS. *"Hello, the Boat!"* New York: Henry Holt and Co., 1938.

DOUGLAS, EMILY TAFT. *Appleseed Farm*. Nashville: Abingdon Press, 1948.

ELMS, FRANCIS RAYMOND. *Let's Explore the Great Lakes*. Chicago: Albert Whitman and Co., 1953.

FAULKNER, NANCY. *The West Is on Your Left Hand*. Garden City: Doubleday & Co., 1953.

FLACK, MARJORIE. *The Boats on the River*. New York: The Viking Press, 1946.

FLETCHER, SIDNEY E. *The Big Book of Indians*. New York: Grosset & Dunlap, 1950.

FOSTER, GENEVIEVE. *Abraham Lincoln*. New York: Charles Scribner's Sons, 1950.

FRIERMOOD, ELISABETH HAMILTON. *Hoosier Heritage*. Garden City: Doubleday & Co., 1954.

GILCHRIST, MARIE E. *The Story of the Great Lakes*. New York: Harper & Brothers, 1942.

GRAHAM, ALBERT POWELL. *La Salle, River Explorer*. Nashville: Abingdon Press, 1954.

HANSEN, HARRY. *The Story of Illinois*. Garden City: Garden City Books, 1956.

HARMER, MABEL. *The True Book of Pioneers*. Chicago: Children's Press, 1957.

HOFSINDE, ROBERT. *Indian Games and Crafts*. New York: William Morrow and Co., 1957.

HOLBERG, RUTH, AND HOLBERG, RICHARD. *Oh Susannah*. Garden City: Doubleday, Doran & Co., 1939.

KELSEY, VERA. *Tomorrow Is for You!* New York: Charles Scribner's Sons, 1953.

LE SUEUR, MERIDEL. *Little Brother of the Wilderness: The Story of Johnny Appleseed*. New York: Alfred A. Knopf, 1947.

McCLOSKEY, ROBERT. *Lentil*. New York: The Viking Press, 1946.

McCORMICK, DELL J. *Paul Bunyan Swings His Axe*. Caldwell, Idaho: The Caxton Printers, 1948.

———. *Tall Timber Tales: More Paul Bunyan Stories*. Caldwell, Idaho: The Caxton Printers, 1951.

McCULLOUGH, JOHN G., AND KESSLER, LEONARD. *Farther and Faster*. New York: Thomas Y. Crowell Co., 1954.

MASON, MIRIAM E. *Caroline and Her Kettle Named Maud*. New York: The Macmillan Co., 1951.

———. *Hominy and His Blunt-nosed Arrow*. New York: The Macmillan Co., 1953.

———. *Little Jonathan*. New York: The Macmillan Co., 1944.

———. *The Middle Sister*. New York: The Macmillan Co., 1947.

———. *Susannah, The Pioneer Cow*. New York: The Macmillan Co., 1944.

MEADOWCROFT, ENID. *By Wagon and Flatboat.* New York: Thomas Y. Crowell Co., 1938.

MEIGS, CORNELIA. *The Willow Whistle.* New York: The Macmillan Co., 1941.

NEUBERGER, RICHARD L. *The Lewis and Clark Expedition.* New York: Random House, 1951.

NOLAN, JEANNETTE C. *George Rogers Clark.* New York: Julian Messner, 1954.

OLDS, ELIZABETH. *Big Fire.* New York: Houghton Mifflin Co., 1945.

OTTO, MARGARET, AND OTTO, STUART. *The Boat and Ship Book.* New York: William Sloane Associates, 1951.

PAYNE, JOSEPHINE B. *The Journey of Josiah Talltatters.* New York: Ariel Books, 1953.

ROUNDS, GLEN. *Ol' Paul the Mighty Logger.* New York: Holiday House, 1936.

SCHNEIDER, HERMAN, AND SCHNEIDER, NINA. *Let's Look under the City.* New York: William R. Scott, Inc., 1954.

STEVENSON, AUGUSTA. *Abe Lincoln, Frontier Boy.* Indianapolis: The Bobbs-Merrill Co., 1932.

———. *Tecumseh, Shawnee Boy.* Indianapolis: The Bobbs-Merrill Co., 1955.

SYME, RONALD. *La Salle of the Mississippi.* New York: William Morrow and Co., 1953.

TURNEY, IDA VIRGINIA. *Paul Bunyan, The Work Giant.* Portland: Binfords & Mort, 1941.

WAGONER, JEAN BROWN. *Jane Addams, Little Lame Girl.* Indianapolis: The Bobbs-Merrill Co., 1957.

WILDER, LAURA INGALLS. *Farmer Boy.* New York: Harper & Brothers, 1953.

———. *Little House in the Big Woods.* New York: Harper & Brothers, 1953.

WILKIE, KATHERINE E. *George Rogers Clark, Boy of the Old Northwest.* Indianapolis: The Bobbs-Merrill Co., 1957.

ZAFFO, GEORGE J. *The Big Book of Real Airplanes.* New York: Grosset & Dunlap, 1951.

FILMS

America's Inland Waterways. Coronet Films. Sound, 13½ minutes, black & white or color.

Beavers. Encyclopaedia Britannica Films. Silent, 15 minutes, black & white.

Birch Bark Canoe. Quebec Publicity Bureau. Sound, 10 minutes, color. *Free loan.*

Chicago. Instructional Films, Inc. Sound, 10 minutes, black & white or color.

The Chicago Fire. Young America Teaching Films. Sound, 27 minutes, black & white.

Detroit—Portrait of a City. Ford Motor Company Film Service. Sound, 25 minutes, color. *Free loan.*

First Flight of the Wright Brothers. Young America Teaching Films. Sound, 27 minutes, black & white.

Flatboatmen of the Frontier. Encyclopaedia Britannica Films. Sound, 10 minutes, black & white.

Illinois. Instructional Films, Inc. Sound, 10 minutes, black & white or color.

Indiana. Instructional Films, Inc. Sound, 10 minutes, black & white or color.

Indian Canoemen. National Film Board of Canada. Sound, 9 minutes, black & white or color.

Iron Ore Mining. Academy Films. Sound, 13 minutes, black & white or color.

La Salle. Encyclopaedia Britannica Films. Sound, 17 minutes, black & white.

Lincoln in Illinois. Illinois State Film Library. Sound, 30 minutes, color. *Free loan.*

Middle States. Encyclopaedia Britannica Films. Sound, 11 minutes, black & white or color.

Minnesota Document. University of Minnesota Audio-Visual Service. Sound, 40 minutes, black & white.

Mississippi River—Upper River. Academy Films. Sound, 14 minutes, black & white or color.

Ohio River—Upper Valley. Academy Films. Sound, 11 minutes, black & white or color.

Our Amazing Beavers. Vermont Development Commission. Sound, 7 minutes, color. *Free loan.*

Paul Bunyan and Johnny Inkslinger. Impco, Inc. Sound, 11 minutes, black & white or color.

Paul Bunyan and the Blue Ox. Coronet Films. Sound, 5½ minutes, black & white or color.

A Pioneer Home. Coronet Films. Sound, 10 minutes, black & white or color.

Pioneers of the Plains. Encyclopaedia Britannica Films. Sound, 11 minutes, black & white.

A Story of Copper. U.S. Bureau of Mines. Sound, 33 minutes, color. *Free loan.*

Woodland Indians of Early America. Coronet Films. Sound, 11 minutes, black & white or color.

FILMSTRIPS

Adventures with Early American Indians. Society for Visual Education, Inc.

Beavers at Home. U.S. Fish and Wildlife Service.

Cattle and the Corn Belt. United World Films.

Chicago, At the Crossroads of a Nation. Eyegate House, Films.

The City Community. Encyclopaedia Britannica Films.

Exploring through Maps. Popular Science Publishing Company.

Flatboatmen of the Frontier. Encyclopaedia Britannica Films.

George Rogers Clark. Encyclopaedia Britannica Films.

History of Our Flag. Young America Films.

Johnny Appleseed. Encyclopaedia Britannica Films.

Lewis and Clark. Young America Films, Inc.

Life in the Early Midwest. Encyclopaedia Britannica Films.

Marquette. Young America Films, Inc.

The Middle States. Encyclopaedia Britannica Films.

The Middle West. Society for Visual Education, Inc.

> *City People of the Middle West*
> *The Corn Belt*
> *East and South of the Corn Belt*
> *Engine Whistles*
> *Singing Wheels*
> *West and North of the Corn Belt*

The Middle West—Its Geography. Popular Science Publishing Company.

The Middle West—Its History. Popular Science Publishing Company.

Paul Bunyan. Encyclopaedia Britannica Films.

Steamboat 'Round the Bend—On the Mississippi. Young America Films, Inc.

The Story of Father Marquette. Society for Visual Education, Inc.

The Wilderness Frontier. Curriculum Films, Inc.

> *Children on the Wilderness Frontier*
> *Community Life on the Wilderness Frontier*
> *The Farm Home of the Wilderness Frontier*
> *Farmers Go West to the Wilderness Frontier*
> *Hunters-Pioneers on the Wilderness Frontier*
> *A New Farm on the Wilderness Frontier*

SONGS

"The Boatman Dance," *America Sings: Stories and Songs of Our Country's Growing.* New York: Alfred A. Knopf.

"The Boatmen's Song," *Work and Sing.* New York: William R. Scott, Inc.

"Indian Children," *The American Singer,* Book II. New York: American Book Co.

"Indian Cradle Song," *The American Singer,* Book III. New York: American Book Co.

"My Bark Canoe," *The American Singer,* Book II. New York: American Book Co.

"Paddy on the Railway," *Songs of Freedom.* New York: Houghton Mifflin Co.

"The Pinery Boy," *Work and Sing.* New York: William R. Scott, Inc.

"Red Iron Ore," *Songs of Freedom.* New York: Houghton Mifflin Co.

"The Shantyman's Life," *America Sings: Stories and Songs of Our Country's Growing.* New York: Alfred A. Knopf.

"Young Abe Lincoln," *The American Singer,* Book III. New York: American Book Co.

RECORDINGS

Birth of Paul Bunyan. Young People's Records, No. 404.

Explorations of Pere Marquette. Enrichment Records, No. 105.

Lewis and Clark. Enrichment Records, No. 105.

Little Hawk—The Indian Boy. Young People's Records, No. 435.

The Little Hero. Young People's Records, No. 9010.

Robert Fulton and the Steamboat. Enrichment Records, No. 112.

The Story of Johnny Appleseed. Walt Disney Productions, No. DBR-60.

Timber-r-r. Young People's Records, No. 504.

Trading Post on the Prairie. Standard School Broadcast Series, No. 6.

The Wright Brothers, Pioneers of Aviation. Enrichment Records, No. 104.

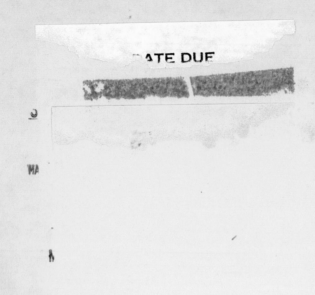